Legend & Lore of
CHAVES COUNTY

North Spring River in Chaves County.
(Historical Society for Southeast New Mexico #287)

LEGEND & LORE OF
CHAVES COUNTY

JOHN LEMAY

DEAD HORSE HISTORY

A SUBSIDIARY OF BICEP BOOKS. ROSWELL, NEW MEXICO

Printed in the United States of America

LeMay, John.
Legend & Lore of Chaves County
ISBN 978-1-953221-01-8
Roswell, Chaves County—Cattle/Ranching/Artesian Water

In memory of Georgia B. Redfield,
one of the greatest Roswell writers and historians.

ROSWELL

The Optic's Special Correspondent Glowingly tells the Tale of the Once Barren Plain, now Made to Blossom as the Rose.

A FERTILE OASIS IN A DESERT

Great Fields of Orchard and Grain Supporting Thousands of Happy Homes.

ETERNAL FOUNTAINS FLOW

Personal Paragraphs and Pertinent Pencilings Penned for the People's Paper,

Las Vegas Daily Optic (August 22, 1900).

A NOTE FROM THE AUTHOR

Growing up, my maternal grandmother gave me a series of books co-authored by her friend, a Roswell historian by the name of Ernestine Chesser Williams. With Professor Emeritus Elvis E. Fleming, also of Roswell, Williams had co-authored a fun little series of volumes entitled *Treasures of History*. There were four in all, and Fleming authored *Treasures of History IV* solo after the passing of Williams. I was quite intrigued by the books in that they offered fantastic stories from Roswell and Chaves County NOT to do with the infamous UFO crash of 1947. They were my introduction to Roswell's "cowboy history" which I thought was exclusive to nearby Lincoln County and its most famous son, Billy the Kid.

Through Williams and Fleming's historical articles, I learned that there was much more to Roswell and Chaves County than UFOs and aliens. And just as you didn't see any UFOs or aliens on the cover of this book, nor will you find them in the pages ahead. This is a book for Chaves County residents, and, in a way, I suppose you could consider this "Treasures V." I mean that in the sense that I tried to find the types of stories that Elvis and Ernestine would have covered were they still with us today, like the once famous but now forgotten holy tortilla of Lake Arthur and other unique area incidents. This book also hinges heavily upon the folklore unearthed by another Roswell writer who preceded Fleming and Williams: Georgia B. Redfield. To say that her output for the Federal Writer's Project of the 1930s was massive would be an understatement, hence this book's dedication to her memory. With no further ado, and in the spirit of those beloved historians, I hope you enjoy *Legend & Lore of Chaves County*.

Artesian well in Chaves County.
(HSSNM #547)

TABLE OF CONTENTS

A Note from the Author...7
Introduction...11

Conquistadors in Chaves County...15
The Cowboy That Time Forgot...17
Van C. Smith's Cosmic Gun Duel...29
Roswell in the Lincoln County War...37
Keeping up with the Joneses...43
Pat Garrett and the Stolen Horses...53
Billy the Kid in Roswell...59
The Man Who Invented Billy the Kid...65
Roswell and the Santa Fe Ring...73
Bottomless Lakes...79
Legend & Lore of Lover's Lane...89
Lorius Lake and the Missing Motorists...95
La Llorona at the Oasis Ranch...99
Old Time Tales of Chihuahuita...105
The Day Roswell was Doomed...111
Legend of Diamond Cave...115
Lily Klasner, the Lady Outlaw...123
Miracles of Saint Mary's...135
Ghosts of WAFB...139
Georgia Redfield's Unmade Movie...145
Lost Evidence in the Pat Garrett Killing...151
Night of the Lechuza...157
Lake Arthur's Holy Tortilla...161

Appendices...165
Bibliography...175
Index...178
About the Author...180

Van Ness Cumming Smith was born to Roswell Smith and his wife Harriett Cummings Smith in Vermont on July 12, 1837. Smith's first scheme of many was to leave home at a young age to pursue the California Gold Rush. Though he didn't strike it rich in California, Smith eventually made a name for himself in Arizona as one of the first settlers of Prescott. Only in his mid-twenties, Smith was still a well-respected man in Arizona Territory and even served as a guide for Joseph Pratt Allyn (associate justice of the territory) when he first entered the area. By 1865, Smith was the first man in the recorded history of Arizona to be appointed Sheriff there, specifically in Yavapai County. In 1868, Smith was in Omaha, Nebraska, where he cemented for himself the reputation of a gentleman gambler. Not too long after that, Smith would found a little place called Roswell...

INTRODUCTION

THE BIRTH OF CHAVES COUNTY

I f one were to sum up the roots of Chaves County in only two words, those words would be water and cattle. James Patterson built a small 15x15 foot adobe trading post in the vicinity of modern-day Roswell specifically because he knew that cattlemen would stop to water their stock at the Hondo River. And while doing so, why not meander over to Patterson's store and buy some supplies. They did, and the little trading post was lucrative enough that it was later bought by Van C. Smith, who expanded it and built an adjoining post office.

Smith was even more successful than Patterson in his endeavor, and soon Smith's place became a notorious gambler's haven. Ash Upson, a writer and early postmaster, described the early days in an 1892 article for the *Roswell Record*:

Van's sporting proclivities could not be suppressed. He had a pack of beagle-hounds, and killed a yearling or two year-old every day to feed them. He made a trip to New York, Philadelphia, Baltimore, Richmond, Va., and other cities and brought back race-horses, game chickens and an un-conquerable bulldog 'Old Crib.' He laid out two parallel half-mile racetracks, now plainly visible, from his store to the Rio Hondo, and built a fantastic judge's stand near the store. His place was visited by dozens of sporting-men from Santa Fe, Las Vegas, Albuquerque, and even from the States. Horse-racing, cock-fighting, dog-fighting, badger-baiting furnished daily amusement, whilst card-playing continued, often, throughout the night. Van was a jovial fellow, big-hearted and generous. Whilst a dozen or two workmen were employed on his buildings, he would call them when a race, or other excitement, was about to take place, and, although they were working by the day, would insist that they quit work and see the fun.

At this usually deserted, lonely, isolated place, a hundred men have assembled, on more than one occasion, and lingered, too, as long as possible; for the temptation was great. The best whiskey and cigars that money would buy, faro, monte, poker and other short card games allured many, and toothsome viands many others. Van had a good housekeeper and a most excellent cook. There was no luxury that money could buy that could not be found at his table.

The first Chaves County Courthouse, constructed in 1889. (HSSNM #747A)

When it came time to name the place in 1872, Smith chose to call it after his father, Roswell Smith. Ironically, many concur that Roswell Smith never set foot in Roswell, though old-time Lincoln County resident Lily Klasner asserted that, "[Van Smith's] father, 'Old Man Smith' lived in a choza on what the local people called *El Loma de Viejo* 'Old Man's Hill'...about two miles northwest of Roswell."

However, despite Klasner's comment, most old-timers and historians alike claimed that the man Roswell was named after never once set foot in the place. As for his son, Van Smith eventually became bored and let his holdings on the property lapse. (Smith neglected one important matter that eventually led to his losing of the property when he forgot to secure a patent for his homestead entry on the land.) He was succeeded by the famous Jones family of Seven Rivers, and they were followed by Captain Joseph C. Lea, regarded by many as the "Father of Roswell" because he actually took the time to cultivate the place into a respectable town.

Captain Lea, far right, standing near an Artesian well. (HSSNM #1888)

In February of 1889, Captain Lea, land developer Charles B. Eddy, and former lawman Pat Garrett journeyed to Santa Fe to petition the creation of two new counties out of then-massive Lincoln County. The result was Eddy and Chaves counties. At the time of its incorporation, the seat of Chaves

County was still relatively small, as Roswell had a population of under 400 people. However, that was soon to change. In the mid-1890s, a Roswellite suffering from a sour stomach due to bad drinking water decided to sink a well on his property. In doing so, he tapped into a huge underground artesian water basin. This brought about an influx of new settlers to the region, which in turn led to the birth of communities that still exist today, like Lake Arthur, Hagerman, and Dexter.

Old time resident Mrs. Mary Neatherlin Dow once remembered that "Roswell was not the place one finds here at the present. Water was peddled around the streets by the barrel. It came from a spring from the bank of North Spring River. For cleaning and washing it was dipped from irrigation ditches." Above is shown North Spring River during an 1893 roundup. (HSSNM #1891)

Like the artesian wells that once gushed into the air, much folklore sprang from the early days of Roswell and Chaves County, including forgotten tales of the likes of Billy the Kid, Pat Garrett, Van Smith, Lily Klasner, and even the ghostly La Llorona. In the pages ahead, you'll find stories of buried treasure, colorful characters, gunfights, mysterious disappearances, and even a few miracles which make up the legend and lore of Chaves County...

1.
CONQUISTADORS IN CHAVES COUNTY

I f there's one area of history that Southeastern New Mexico seemed to miss out on, it was that of the conquistadors who first explored what would become New Mexico. After Hernán Cortés conquered the Aztec Empire around 1520, the Spaniards were eager to see what awaited them to the north. One of the first to explore North America was Álvar Núñez Cabeza de Vaca, a survivor of a 1527 shipwreck off the coast of Florida. He and several companions wandered the Southwest for eight years until they made their way back to Mexico. Some have wondered how close Cabeza de Vaca ever came to current-day Chaves County in the year 1536. One historian, Cleve Hallenbeck, thought it was likely Cabeza de Vaca came near where Artesia is today along the Pecos.

In the current-day vicinity of Bottomless Lakes State Park is a petroglyph depicting what appears to be a conquistador. The simple figure is that of a man on a horse, and the best guess that historians can offer is that it depicted Antonio de Espejo, who came down the Pecos in the year 1583. One historian who put a great deal of thought into the route of the Espejo expedition via the rivers they described was Morgan Nelson, who appropriately served as the Chaves County Flood Commissioner on several occasions.

In a report on Spanish explorers in Southeastern New Mexico, Nelson also alluded to the glyphs, writing, "There is some evidence from some markings on caves that some

Spanish people came through here later but no one stayed or wrote about it." Nelson also mused as to why none of the Spanish explorers, like Espejo, never "reported having seen [Roswell's] Spring Rivers. Surely they would be worthy of reporting as they were such an unusual phenomenon in this dry country."[1]

North Spring River, which the conquistadors somehow missed during their explorations. (HSSNM #568B)

In *Leading Facts of New Mexican History*, Ralph Emerson Twitchell also pondered this conundrum:

> It seems strange, however, if the army crossed the Pecos in the neighborhood of Roswell, that the beautiful streams of water near that place, and the springs, also different from the brackish water of the Pecos, are not mentioned by Castaneda. I incline to the belief that the army crossed the Pecos further north than Roswell, else the Spring Rivers would have been noticed and mentioned."[2]

The mystery of the absence of the Spring Rivers aside, for certain two groups of conquistadors did explore what is now Chaves County. The first was the Espejo expedition, of which Diego Pérez de Luxán kept a detailed journal of the route.

After exploring the northern portion of New Mexico and to return to Mexico, the group decided to travel south down the Pecos. As such, they certainly traversed current day Chaves County. Nelson examined the journal and added educated guesses as to where the expedition was in relation to Chaves County. In one entry, Luxán noted marching "through marshy land along the river" which they called El Salado "because the river is more salty here than before, on account of the brackish water from the many springs that empty into it." Nelson noted that this was most likely the present location of Salt Creek, north of Rowell.

After traveling south through about ten miles of "mini marshes," they came to another place that they called El Ancon de la Laguna "because of a lagoon formed at a bay near the river." Nelson speculated that, most likely, they were now either at Bitter Lakes or one of the northernmost Bottomless Lakes, even though they mentioned neither the Pecos River bluffs nor any lakes themselves. After marching through what is now Roswell, they arrived 20 miles south to what was most likely the Hagerman area, although curiously they did not mention the Felix River. They called the new place El Mosquital due to the many mosquitoes in the marshy area.

Frederic Remington's depiction of Coronado's expedition.

After Espejo came Gaspar Castaño de Sosa. The purpose of his expedition was to establish the first colony or village of new Spain in New Mexico. He set out in July of 1590 with 170 people in a caravan that consisted of crude two-wheeled carts, which historian Elvis Fleming speculated were likely the first type of wheeled vehicles to roll their way across Texas and New Mexico. By December 3, 1590, the caravan reached the vicinity of Hagerman, camping in sand dunes as they traveled parallel to the Pecos River. On December 6, they endured a prairie fire wherein "the savanna caught fire, so that it was thought that one of the carts would be burned." Eventually, they put out the fire and camped next on the northeast bank of the Pecos, a little ways north of what would later be Oasis Dairy. By December 8, they had moved upstream past the mouth of the Hondo in "the vicinity of the present highway 380 bridge east of Roswell."[3] Fleming speculated that "when they went to some little ravines to sleep," it was probably in the vicinity of Bitter Lakes or Salt Creek. After that, they moved on to a grove of cottonwood trees, most likely Bosque Grande, which would later become the headquarters for John Chisum. They noted that "in these places was a very great quantity of mesquite (beans), and if it had not been for this, very great difficulty would have been suffered." By December 10, they were out of the confines of Chaves County and proceeded to Pecos Pueblo, where they arrived on December 31st.

Those two brief expeditions comprised Chaves County's connection to the conquistadors. As to why none chose to settle here, Nelson speculated, "Perhaps the wild Apache Indians caused the Spanish to avoid this place."[4]

Chapter Notes

[1] Nelson, "The Early Spanish Through the Middle Pecos," p.5.
[2] Twitchell, *Leading Facts of New Mexican History*, p.229.
[3] Fleming, *Treasures of History II*, p.5.
[4] Nelson, "The Early Spanish Through the Middle Pecos," p.5.

2.
THE COWBOY
THAT TIME FORGOT

Historically speaking, Captain Joseph C. Lea is credited as the "Father of Roswell." Though he certainly wasn't the area's first settler, he earned the title because he was the first man to try and cultivate Roswell as a town. However, when it comes to the man who truly started Roswell, that would be James Patterson, a cattleman often relegated to the footnotes of history. Patterson was quite a trailblazer who drove a herd of cattle into New Mexico from Texas before Oliver Loving and Charles Goodnight. Prior to this, Patterson had been a beef contractor for Fort Sumner and also Fort Stanton during the Civil War. More importantly to this volume, where today stands Pioneer Plaza in Roswell, nearly 160 years ago, Patterson recognized the spot as an excellent place to build a small 15x15 foot adobe trading post. The area was prime real estate as we would call it today due to its proximity to the Hondo and Spring Rivers that used to flow abundantly through the region. Because of this, many cattle drivers stopped to water their herds in this area.

To digress, Patterson was born in Ohio in 1833 but grew up in Illinois. He came to New Mexico in his mid-twenties in either 1859 or 1860, according to Morgan Nelson in "First Among the First: James Patterson, 1833-1892." Nelson explained, "[Patterson] may have been a soldier in the 7th U.S. Cavalry and mustered out here prior to the Civil War, however, sockman and rancher Robert K. Wylie reported he had worked for Patterson in Palestine, Anderson County, Texas."[1] According to records listed in Indian Depredation Case #5622, written in 1898, Patterson came to New Mexico Territory sometime prior to the Civil War and there worked "putting in wood, hay, and everything for the government then."

Portion of old Fort Sumner, which today no longer exists.

As stated earlier, it was during the Civil War that Patterson firmly gained a foothold in the cattle trade of New Mexico by supplying beef to Fort Stanton and Fort Sumner, beginning in 1864. It was Patterson who realized that he could drive cattle herds from Texas into New Mexico to the newly established Bosque Redondo in Fort Sumner, where thousands of Navajo had been relocated after enduring the Long Walk. Patterson entered into a partnership with Captain Thomas Roberts, formerly of the California Column, and another rancher, William C. Franks, to begin the cattle-driving venture. For the span of exactly one year, from September 1865 to the end of August 1866, Patterson held an exclusive contract with the army to drive cattle to Fort Sumner.

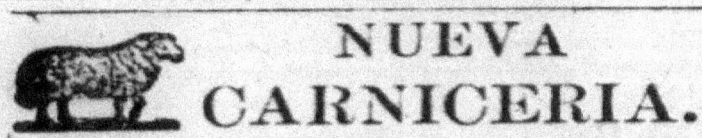

NUEVA CARNICERIA.
......

El abajo firmado participa al público que ha establecido y abierto en Santa Fé una nueva carnicería en la calle d · San Francisco una puerta al poniente del Salon "Star of the West," en cuyo local siempre tendrá de venta la mejor clase de

CARNE DE RES,
CARNE DE CARNERO,
CARNE DE TERNERO,
CARNE DE MARRANO,
Etc., Etc.,

Y espera recibir de los convecinos una porcion liberal de su patrocinio.
JAMES PATTERSON.

Spanish language ad for James Patterson in the *Santa Fe New Mexican* that ran in the late 1860s.

It was in Fort Sumner that Patterson met Pitzer Chisum, brother of the famous John Chisum, who had yet to gain a foothold in New Mexico. Pitzer worked for Patterson for a time, then returned to Texas and reported to brother John the need for cattle in New Mexico. Later, it was Patterson who eventually sold Chisum some land north of Roswell called Bosque Grande ("Big Woods"), which was the cattleman's first base of operations in Chaves County before moving to South Springs—also sold to Chisum by Patterson. As already stated, considering that Patterson made his first big drive into New Mexico in 1865, he preceded the famous Goodnight-Loving Cattle Trail to follow. In the words of Morgan Nelson, "It would appear that Goodnight and Loving heard of the success Patterson was having and promptly joined in; but the trail they took was not as mysterious or as unknown as some writers would have us believe."[2]

As proof of this statement, Nelson reproduced a letter dictated on September 2, 1865, which stated that cattle drives from Texas into New Mexico had "already been twice successfully accomplished by Mr. Patterson" and that it was hopefully the beginning of "a great and profitable trade."[3]

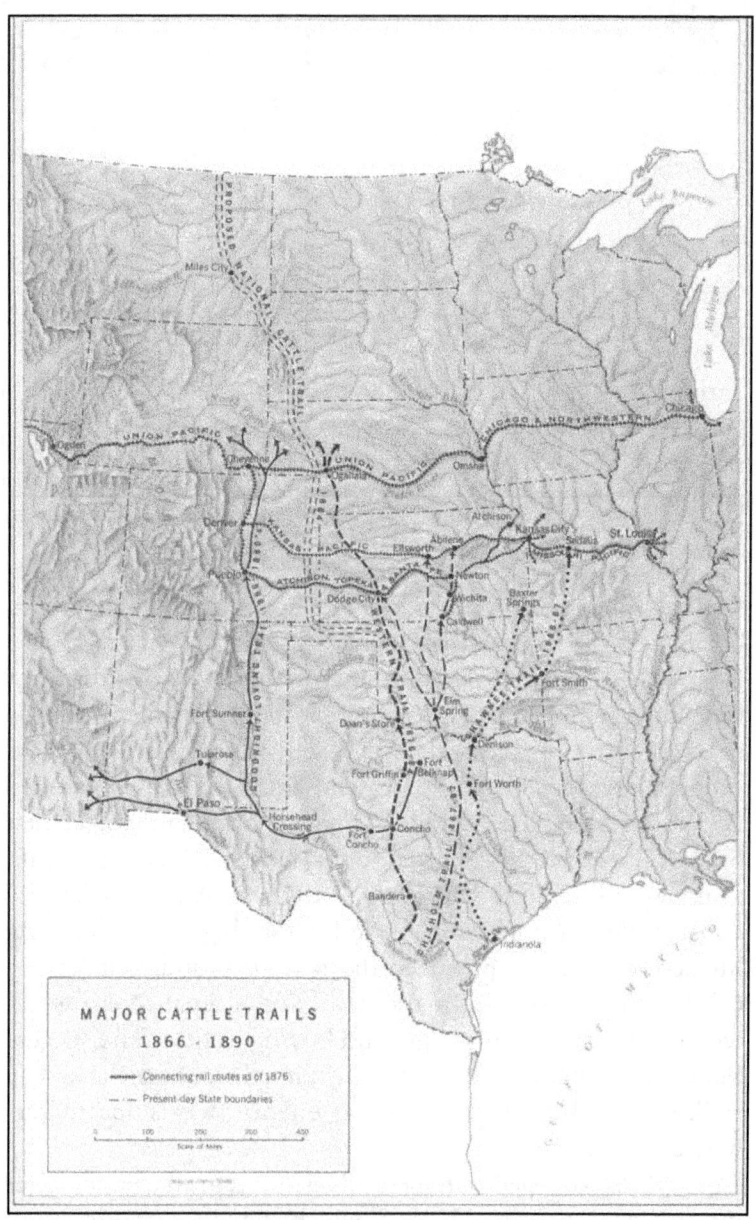

Goodnight-Loving Trail Map. (National Parks Service)

The *Santa Fe New Mexican* of April 19, 1869, also sang Patterson's praises and seemed to be trying to induce him to run for the Territorial Legislature.[4] It stated:

> Colonel James Patterson, one of the live men of this Territory, it still in the city on one of his transient business visits. We are happy to know of the prosperity in business of our enterprising and public spirited citizens such as Col. Patterson is showing himself to be, for their prosperity is the public prosperity and the public welfare. Patterson has peers among us in pecuniary ability, but his peers in progressive spirit and enterprise we fear are too few and too far between. What we want is more Jim Pattersons in New Mexico!

Chisum's long house. (HSSNM #1564-63)

As stated before, it was sometime in the late 1860s, likely 1866, that Patterson begat his trading post along the Hondo, which he eventually sold to Van C. Smith. Around this time, John Chisum was operating predominantly out of Bosque Grande, north of current-day Roswell. Patterson had acquired some ranchland near the South Spring River in either 1873 or 1874 from a rancher named J.M. Hudson. Patterson, who was said to owe $7,000 to Chisum, then turned around and sold the new ranchland to Chisum, thus repaying his debt and making a profit in the process. And with that, Patterson had effectively moved two of Roswell's most prominent players into the region.

After selling the trading post to Smith, Patterson went from being a cattleman to a prospector and sometimes gunfighter. During this wild time, it is known that he acquired a wife, Sadie M. Patterson, and had two children with her, though records of the marriage are harder to pin down when compared to Patterson's mining ventures.[5] Patterson was next found in the middle of a gold mining venture and a murder in Georgetown, New Mexico, in 1880. On February 23, 1880, Patterson killed a man named John Powers and was tried for the death in the years to follow. So the story went, Powers owed Patterson money and the killing naturally took place inside of a saloon. Patterson had invited Powers to drink with him, and when he didn't after several invitations, Patterson became enraged. A shouting match followed, and Patterson soon shot Powers.

According to the court report of the incident:

> Testimony brought out that the crime's setting was Johnson's Saloon in Georgetown. John Powers was playing cards, and Patterson approached the table and invited Powers to drink with him. Powers refused and Patterson left. An hour later Patterson returned and invited all present to drink with him. Powers again refused, whereupon Patterson was reported to have said: "Then you don't like me, you damned son of a bitch!" Words passed and Powers started for the door saying, "You will have to take this out of me!"

Powers was referring to money that he owed Patterson, a fact that the court later recognized. Furthermore, Powers had threatened Patterson's life numerous times in the past. Therefore, when Patterson drew his pistol, followed Powers out the door, shot him twice, and Powers "fell in the street mortally wounded," the court considered the killing to be semi-justified. Or, that is to say, Patterson was convicted of fourth-degree murder, for which he was sentenced to only one year in jail in 1882. (As an interesting aside, Patterson's neck was saved from the hangman's noose by none other than famous lawyer Colonel Albert J. Fountain, who would famously vanish crossing White Sands in 1896.)

—Mr. James Patterson came up from the White Oaks yesterday. He reports the camp booming, and at least $100,000 worth of ore on the dump of the Homestake—such ore as was never before seen in New Mexico.

Prior to Patterson's 1882 sentencing, it would appear that he moved on to White Oaks, another gold boomtown, after the killing of Powers. The October 29, 1880 edition of the *Las Vegas Gazette* reported that he was one of two "principal saloon keepers" with William Hudgens. Presumably, this clipping from the *Las Vegas Gazette* of January 1, 1881, refers to the same James Patterson.

After completing his one-year sentence in jail in 1883, Patterson's whereabouts were nebulous for the next decade. He next appeared in the papers in 1890, which listed him as having just taken a long overdue return trip to his birthplace in Ohio.[6] It also listed him as living in the Gold Hill mining district near Silver City. He resurfaced in the newspapers in 1892—not a good year for him. Patterson was still in the mining business, and the *Sierra County Advocate* of January 15, 1892, reported how Patterson was having difficulties with "Coleman, the Gold Hill mill man, over Patterson's right to have the dies in the mine lifted after his ore was run." As it turned out, poor Patterson had more or less been swindled out of 25 tons of ore from the mine, which amounted to all of a $5 profit for him in the end. Patterson's next appearance in the newspapers was better. On August 2, 1892, the *Southwest Sentinel* reported that his Gold Hill property, the Reservation Mine, had made a "rich strike" and "was now producing seven ounces of gold per ton."

However, a few days later, Patterson's obituary was printed in the August 9th edition of the *Southwest Sentinel*. It reported how Patterson was attacked at his home by a drunken and disgruntled worker named Esequel Mena. For context, Mena had previously been a part of the Revolt of La Ascensión, Chihuahua, a political uprising that had taken place at the small, aforementioned village early in 1892. Mena had apparently escaped northward to begin working in the mines of the Gold Hill region, specifically for Patterson.

Chihuahua Hill.   SILVER CITY. New Mexico.

It was around 9 PM when Mena spotted his boss at Snyder's Saloon and asked if he'd purchase a bottle of whiskey for him, to which Patterson obliged. However, a bit later, Mena asked Patterson to buy him four more bottles, to which he declined.[7] Patterson left the saloon with a friend, Idus L. Fielder, and began walking back to Patterson's home, where both men's families awaited. Mena and several other men followed the duo there and began an argument in the front yard, getting between Patterson and his front door. A shoving match ensued, but eventually Patterson and Fielder got inside the house, and the small gang departed. Inside, they armed themselves and then decided to go out to the corral to make sure the ruffians had not stolen their horses. They were relieved to see the horses still there, but upon returning to the house, Mena was back.

A QUEER STORY.

A Double Murder in Grant County— But Nobody will Be Hanged For It.

Last Saturday evening a Mexican shot and mortally wounded James Patterson, and Patterson, after hav'ng been shot through the body, killed the murderer. This occurred at Gold Hill, Grant county. Idus L. Fielder, a friend of Patterson, had just delivered a campaign address to the miners of the camp, and he and Patterson were en route to the latter's home when the Mexican stopped them and asked for a drink of liquor. Patterson ordered the bartender to give the man a drink and passed on. Later the Mexican followed Patterson and Fielder home and began firing at them. Fielder loaned Patterson his revolver and a battle ensued. The Mexican fired three shots, one of which took effect in Patterson's side, passing entirely through his body. The ball went through the liver and the lower portion of the lungs. After receiving this mortal wound Patterson opened fire on the Mexican and shot him through the heart, killing him instantly. Patterson died on Sunday. He leaves a wife and two children. The Mexican is said to be one of the mob which killed Ancheta in Mexico several months ago.

The *Santa Fe New Mexican* of August 11, 1892.

"Mr. Patterson, Mr. Patterson!" Fielder cried. "My God, he is breaking into the house!" Mena, hearing the cry, turned and aimed his pistol at Patterson. "Patterson, defend yourself, he has a pistol!" Fielder shouted, and Patterson and Mena fired at one another simultaneously.[8] Patterson fired twice, getting Mena first in the hand and then the heart with a killing shot. Mena fired three shots at Patterson, one of which ripped through his stomach. The wounded Patterson was assisted into his home by Fielder, and doctors were sent for from Deming and Silver City. However, Patterson knew it was futile and that soon he would die. In his final hours, Patterson made certain that his last will and testament was to his wishes. He lasted until 5 PM Sunday before finally expiring. A few weeks later, the papers reported that Patterson's Gold Hill mine had closed down but would hopefully reopen after his affairs had been cleared up. If they ever were or not has been lost to the sands of time. As for Patterson, he was buried in the Gold Hill Cemetery with a headstone reading, "He is not dead but sleepeth."

Chapter Notes

[1] Nelson, "First Among the First," *WWHA Journal* (October 2009), p.3.

[2] Ibid, p.4.

[3] Ibid, p.5.

[4] The blurb was listed, coincidentally, underneath an ad for Colonel J. Francisco Chaves, who Chaves County would later be named for.

[5] Sadie M. Patterson was listed as his late wife in the *Lordsburg Liberal* of April 7, 1893.

[6] *Las Vegas Daily Optic* (August 7, 1890).

[7] According to the *Carlsbad Current Argus* of August 20, 1892, Mena first asked Patterson for $5 which he claimed he was owed in wages. Unsure of whether this was true or not, Patterson declined. When Mena next asked for a bottle of whiskey, Patterson obliged, and that was the end of it.

[8] In the version of the fight presented in the *Carlsbad Current Argus* of August 20, 1892, Mena fired three times first, hitting Patterson. The wounded Patterson then fired two shots, one of which went through Mena's heart, killing him. As for Patterson, in this version, he lasted until Monday as opposed to Sunday.

3.
VAN C. SMITH's
COSMIC GUN DUEL

Ever since its rendezvous with a UFO in 1947, Roswell has become synonymous with all things otherworldly. Perhaps it's appropriate then that one of Roswell's founders was involved in what the papers considered to be a cosmically induced gun duel. A few years after establishing Roswell, Van C. Smith let his holdings lapse, some say out of boredom. Whatever the cause, Smith moved on to the much livelier town of Santa Fe, where he carved out a niche for himself as a man about town and a casino owner. For instance, the *Santa Fe New Mexican* of May 24, 1876, gave a glowing description of Smith's property, writing, "On this stream is the handsome residence of Van C. Smith, and I think the Gov. will bear me out in the assertion, that during his travel in New Mexico, he saw no more delightful natural location."

A few weeks later, Smith was in the papers for more sensational and scandalous reasons. On June 20th, the papers said he engaged in a "strange" gun duel and "much promiscuous shooting in one of the most frequented thoroughfares and densely populated portions of Santa Fe." The duel in Santa Fe Plaza was described as strange for several reasons. Smith was drinking in a local saloon when he and a friend became at odds with one another until they decided to settle matters in a gun fight. Strangely, Smith brought a rifle to the duel instead of a revolver, and he and his opponent didn't follow the proper protocol before they began firing at one another in the streets. Neither man was mortally wounded, and both lived to fight another day. In fact, they even reconciled their friendship after the Attorney General dropped the charges against the duo for endangering the citizens of Santa Fe later that year.

However, the oddest thing about the incident was the fact that the papers claimed the strange duel was induced by cosmic forces. As it was, an early-day meteorologist, Professor John H. Tice, had recently made waves in the papers by claiming that the summer equinox of June 20th was destined to be tumultuous. Tice had risen to prominence the previous year when he published a weather almanac that became popular among farmers. Because Tice had a knack for predicting the weather at a time when meteorology was very hit and miss, newspapers were usually eager to print his predictions. Tice, it should also be noted, predicted the weather by way of the planets. Specifically, he followed Mercury and the non-existent planet Vulcan, which many astronomers believed in prior to the 20th century.

Santa Fe Plaza bustling with activity c.1885.

Of the looming summer solstice, the *Blue Rapids Times* of June 15, 1876, noted:

In consequence of the earth passing through the solar node, that is through the electric stratum projected into space in the plane of the sun's equator, the solar nodal disturbances, as well as the equinoxes may manifest more than ordinary energy.

Prof. Tice says that in consequence of the earth passing through the solar node, that is, through the electric stratum projected into space in the plane of the sun's equator, the solar nodal disturbances, as well as the equinoxes, may manifest more than ordinary energy.

WEATHER FORECASTS FOR JUNE.
Disturbing causes will occur:
June 3.—Vulcan at solar node 80°.
9.—Vulcan's equinox at 170°.
11.—Earth at solar node 260°.
12.—Mercury at solar node 260°.
15.—Vulcan at solar node 260°.
20.—Vulcan at equinox 350°.
23.—Venus at solar node 260°.
26.—Vulcan at solar node 80°.
The most energetic disturbances are the equinoxes occurring June 9th and 20th.

Clippings related to Professor Tices's weather predictions of 1876.

Likewise, in another paper, Tice predicted that due to the planet Vulcan, "The most energetic disturbances are the equinoxes occurring June 9th and 20th." This was likely why when Smith engaged in his bizarre gun duel on June 20th that the Santa Fe papers decided to link it to the much-ballyhooed cosmic storm.

Harper's Weekly Illustration of the Soldier's Monument by Clarence Pullen.

Otherworldly forces or not, Smith was enjoying some day-drinking at a local watering hole where he was visiting with Joseph Stinson.[1] (Not much is known of Stinson other than that he was a Santa Fe businessman comparable to Smith in terms of social status, and several articles identified him as a saloon owner himself.) At some point during their meeting, an argument occurred, which produced some "harsh language."

The *Santa Fe New Mexican* of June 21st reported, "Both parties were very much under the influence of liquor at the time, and to settle the difficulty, Stinson proposed to Smith to meet him at the monument in the Plaza, and fight it out the old way, with pistols." Smith and Stinson went their separate ways to procure pistols for the duel, only Smith decided to grab a Winchester rifle. Stinson arrived at the Plaza first, at 5 PM, where he waited for Smith. When he saw Smith approaching with a rifle rather than a revolver, he became alarmed and "commenced blazing away at long range, before Smith reached the gate."

The *Santa Fe New Mexican* continued,

> Having emptied his revolver, Stinson leisurely walked across the center of the Plaza, to the west, and entered the drug store of Dr. John E. Murphy, Smith firing one or more shots from the Winchester. In this strange duel Smith received two severe, but we are pleased to say, not dangerous wounds, and Stinson escaped without so much as a scratch. One of the balls entered the palm of Mr. Smith's right hand, coming out above the wrist, and the other lodged in his right hip. There are conflicting accounts about Smith's firing, some contending that he fired one or more shots, and others that he did not discharge his piece.

The paper stated that their reporter arrived at the scene after hearing gunshots and cries of "Joe Stinson and Van Smith are shooting at each other in the Plaza!" Upon arrival outside of the Governor's palace, the reporter said he saw,

> Mr. Smith standing on the east side of the Soldiers' Monument in the center of the Plaza, holding a Winchester 16-shooter at rest, as if waiting for someone, all alone, with blood streaming from one of his hands. Col. Willison was the first to reach him, and next came Gov. Arny;[2] to the latter Smith gave up his gun and was led over to his room at the Broad Gauge saloon, and Dr. Gordon immediately summoned to his assistance. Going along with the crowd, we saw blood freely sprinkled about the middle eastern gate of the Plaza, and one of the palings of the fence shattered by a bullet. ... Proceeding again to the monument in the Plaza, we found blood spattered on its eastern front and the indentation of a bullet in the granite panel, high upon its northeastern corner, and also the mark of a glancing bullet in its southeastern corner.

The paper puzzled over the fact that both men were regarded as "quiet, peaceable citizens" and that their friends were shocked that "such men could plan and carry out so desperate an engagement in the very heart of the city, whether drunk or sober, where the lives of so many disinterested persons were endangered."

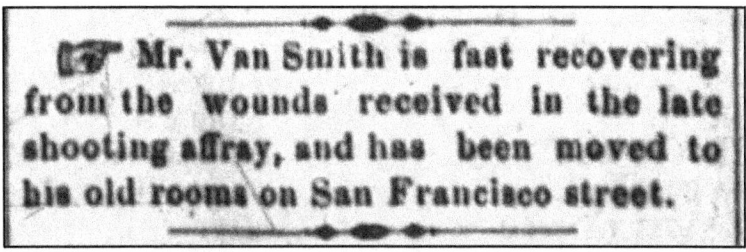

Mr. Van Smith is fast recovering from the wounds received in the late shooting affray, and has been moved to his old rooms on San Francisco street.

Weekly New Mexican of July 4, 1876.

The *Santa Fe New Mexican* said that both men were interviewed the next morning of the 21st and were already back on friendly terms. Stinson, it was said, deeply regretted the "unfortunate turn of an engagement made under the excitement of liquor and without malicious motives." Smith, on the other hand, claimed not to remember some of the events, possibly due to so much drinking. Specifically, Smith claimed that he did not "recollect anything about pistols being specified..." In his thinking, the plan was to meet Stinson in the plaza and proceed from there to find a "more secluded trysting-place" for their duel.

"[Smith] was resting easy under Dr. Gordon's treatment, and with continued good care expects soon to be on the streets again," it said. What's most interesting, though, was the *New Mexican's* concluding paragraph:

> The long continued dry spell of weather and the unusual flow of electricity in yesterday's atmosphere, seemed to have caused a more general warlike desire than usual. We are working out the particulars of several knockdowns said to have occurred.

It's debatable if the papers really believed that cosmic forces were to blame and were possibly just making light of the event since no one was killed. One also has to wonder if the duo's lawyers used that to their advantage when the issue was taken to court. Probably not, and, in any case, the charges against the two were dismissed in September. However, one can't deny the irony that the founder of Roswell got in a gun duel that the media blamed on a cosmic storm.

> ☞ In the Rio Arriba District Court on Wednesday, in the case of the Territory against Joseph Stinson and Van C. Smith for fighting a duel, the evidence not being sufficient to convict, the suit was withdrawn by the Attorney General, and the defendants discharged. Both have returned to their homes.

The Santa Fe New Mexican of September 22, 1876.

Chapter Notes

[1] Stinson was the star of another odd episode reported in the *Santa Fe New Mexican* of October 27, 1880. In "A Story of a Ring," Stinson was departing a saloon that he owned when he literally bumped into a passerby on the street. In doing so, he accidentally dropped a precious diamond ring into the man's pocket which he later retrieved in a humorous manner. By chance, Stinson encountered the man again the next day and asked the man if he would be so good as to check his pockets for him. The man produced the ring, which he had no idea that he was carrying.

[2] It should be noted that Samuel Axtell was governor at this time, and the "Gov. Arny" referred to was likely William Frederick Milton Arny, who served as secretary of state in New Mexico from 1862-1867. In 1876, he represented New Mexico at the Centennial Exposition and was likely in Santa Fe on business relating to that.

4.
ROSWELL IN THE LINCOLN COUNTY WAR

I f one ever wonders why Roswell isn't mentioned more often regarding the infamous Lincoln County War, that's because Roswell was neutral. For those that need a brief refresher, the war lasted from February of 1878 until July of that same year. There were several gunfights in the "war," the most famous of which began on July 15, 1878. Over the course of five days, both sides fired at one another in the streets of Lincoln until the home of Alexander McSween was set on fire and burned to the ground, more or less ending the war.

At its core, the conflict was a feud between opposing political factions. On the one side were wealthy cattle baron John Chisum, lawyer Alexander McSween, and English rancher John Tunstall. On the opposing side were Lawrence G. Murphy and his partner, James J. Dolan, who ran a mercantile together in Lincoln. The reason for the conflict was two-fold. Murphy and Dolan hated Chisum because he was their competitor in the cattle trade, as both parties wanted the lucrative government beef contract to supply cattle to nearby Fort Stanton. Murphy and Dolan also hated Chisum's friend Tunstall, who opened a general store in direct competition with Murphy's, which was the only other major mercantile in Lincoln and was called "The House."

View of the village of Lincoln. (HSSNM #1546)

That Roswell wasn't privy to the violence of the war was celebrated at the time. Ironically, today, had Roswell hosted any battles related to the war, such incidents could have served as another avenue for tourism. In an article that appeared years later in the April 29, 1892 edition of the *Roswell Record*, former postmaster Ash Upson explained how the peace was kept in Roswell:

> The immediate vicinity of Roswell knew nothing of the fight, except by rumor, until the summer of 1877. F.G. Christie, assistant postmaster under George R. Smith, brother of Van C. Smith, was charged, unjustly perhaps, with tampering with Chisum's mail. Chisum applied for and secured a commission as postmaster to his book-keeper, M.A. Upson, who remained in charge of the office from Aug. 1st 1877, throughout the dark days, and succeeded in weathering the fierce storms, and converting the post office and its environs, into neutral ground, upon which the adherents of either parties, sworn enemies, met, peacefully to all outward seeming.

The secret was that the postmaster warned them all that so soon as the first broil occurred, the first gun fired, or the premises, in any manner, made the scene of battle, he would at once send in his resignation to Washington, and his post office paraphernalia to Fort Stanton. Honest men, who were fighting, as they believed, for their rights, their adherents, on both sides, rustlers (thieves) from Colorado, Arizona, Texas, and other localities, depended upon the post office at Roswell for their intercourse with the world outside, a very dangerous circle, and could not afford to risk its suspicion. Hence the postmaster and post office were respected by both factions. The result was—as stated in the previous letter, that never during the years when Roswell was the center of an immense battlefield rampant with anarchy, murder, arson, incendiarism, robbery and worse,—not a shot was fired in malice or anger within four miles of Roswell.[1]

The war kicked off in February of 1878 when John Tunstall was famously gunned down and killed by a group of cowboys aligned with Murphy and Dolan. To avenge him, a constable's posse was formed consisting of area cowboys loyal to Tunstall, among them Billy the Kid. They called themselves the Regulators and in their travels down the lower Pecos in early March, they came across members of the group that killed Tunstall. Among them, they managed to arrest William S. "Buck" Morton and Frank Baker, whom Billy the Kid was said to try and kill on the spot but was restrained.

On their way to Lincoln, the group stopped by John Chisum's South Spring Ranch on the night of March 8th. There, Morton dictated a letter to a Virginia attorney and also his sweetheart, according to the diary of John Chisum's niece, Sallie. The next day, the Regulators brought the two prisoners through Roswell where they crossed paths with postmaster Upson, who would later adapt this encounter into *The Authentic Life of Billy the Kid*.[2] Upson wrote how "Morton with the rest of the party, was well known to the postmaster, M.A. Upson, and Morton requested him should any important event transpire, to write to his cousin and inform him of the facts connected therewith."[3] William Brent, the son of James Brent, a notable Lincoln County pioneer, recollected in his book, *The Complete and Factual Life of Billy the Kid*, the following specifics of a conversation between Upton and Morton:

> Ash replied to Morton, "You looking for anything to happen?"
>
> Morton responded he wasn't, "But if something goes wrong I want my people to know about it."
>
> McCloskey [one of the posse members] said to Morton in a low voice, "If they try to harm you, they'll have to get me first."
>
> Upson said he noticed the Kid glance significantly at other posse members at McCloskey's words."[4]

Illustration of the Kid gunning down Morton and Baker.

Before leaving, according to author Frazier Hunt in *The Tragic Days of Billy the Kid*, Upson told the posse that Governor Samuel Axtell had just issued a proclamation in Fort Stanton that resulted in the Regulators no longer being a legitimate posse. Upson should have known that telling the Regulators of this new development would surely sign Morton and Baker's death certificates. As the men left the post office, surely Upson knew that the prisoner's fates weren't good. Upson and the by-now-late Morton's suspicions were confirmed when Frank

McNab walked into the Roswell post office on the 11th and told him that the two prisoners had been killed. As requested, Upson immediately mailed off Morton's letter. Upson also used McNab's account to write a piece for the Mesilla *Independent,* which was published on March 16th. According to McNab:

> When we had ridden some 20 miles and had reached a point some 5 or 6 miles from Black Water, Morton was riding side by side with one of the posse, McCloskey, when he suddenly snatched McCloskey's pistol from the scabbard and shot him dead.
>
> Although mounted on a slow horse, he put him to his best speed closely followed by Frank Baker. They were speedily overtaken and killed.[5]

What really happened was revealed to J. Evetts Haley by a member of the posse, Florencio Chavez, in 1927, though. Chavez claimed that a member of their posse, William McCloskey, was suspected of being a turncoat. One of the posse asked McCloskey, "How is the best way to kill those s.o.b.s?" (the aforementioned s.o.b.s being Morton and Baker, of course). When McCloskey replied that they should still take them to jail and leave it to the law, in the minds of the Regulators, it confirmed their suspicions. Immediately after hearing McCloskey's answer, Jim French and Henry Brown rode up to McCloskey and shot him. The prisoners, Morton and Baker, took this as a logical cue to make a run for it on their horses and were shot by the Regulators.

There was another slight flare-up in Roswell on July 1, 1878, shortly before the culmination of the war during the Five-Day Siege.[6] When John Chisum's brother, Pitzer, stopped at Captain Lea's house for a visit, some scalawags from the Dolan crowd were hiding outside. Their plan was to capture Pitzer, brand him with Chisum's Long Rail brand, and then slit his ears in a jingle-bob! (The jingle-bob, by the way, referred to the way Chisum spliced the ears of his cattle down the middle.) Their nefarious plan never panned out, however, due to some

Pitzer Chisum.

well-staged trickery on the part of Lea, who helped Pitzer slip away unnoticed. A few days later on July 4th, Upson saw William Bonney, currently visiting Chisum's ranch, when he paid a visit to the Roswell store. With him were two other "stars" of the war, the Coe brothers, Frank and George, along with other assorted Regulators (even though they were now "unofficial" they kept the name). On the group's way back to South Springs, they were chased by twelve men from a Seven Rivers posse, guns blazing all the way to Chisum's ranch.

According to the late Dusty Huckabee of Roswell, when Billy came racing up to the ranch, Sallie Chisum was outside hanging up her bloomers to dry on the clothesline. According to folklore heard by Huckabee, the Dolan men fired some shots and put a few holes in poor Sallie's bloomers! Fortunately, neither Sallie, the Kid, nor anyone was hurt, and it was the liveliest that the Roswell area ever got during the war.[7]

Chapter Notes

[1] Upson, "Roswell: Something More of Its History During Troublous Times," *Roswell Record* (April 29, 1892). [HSSNM Archives, Patterson Collection, Box 1.]
[2] Though credited to Pat Garrett, Upson wrote most of the book.
[3] Upson/Garrett, *Authentic Life* (Annotated Ed. by Frederick Nolan), p.59.
[4] Brent, *Factual Life,* p.55.
[5] Hunt, *Tragic Days,* pp.45-46.
[6] Adams, *Three Ranches West,* p.478.
[7] The author heard this story by way of Dusty's friend, Dewey Johnson, who said Dusty had heard it from the likes of Peter Hurd and other Lincoln County residents.

5.
KEEPING UP WITH THE JONESES

The Jones Family of Seven Rivers are legend in Southeastern New Mexico. It's no wonder why Eddy County, to the south of Chaves County, proudly lays claim to them. It was at Seven Rivers, where "cowboys could read newspapers in the dark" thanks to constant gunfire, that the Joneses settled and ran a trading post that was renowned across the Southwest. The family comprised of patriarch Heiskell Jones, matriarch Barabra "Ma'am" Jones, and their ten children—the best-known of which was Lincoln County War fighter John Jones. The family was immortalized in Eve Ball's beloved book *Ma'am Jones of the Pecos*. Though written in the style of a historical novel, with much presumed dialogue, the book still presented a very accurate history of the family. This is because Ball compiled it by interviewing as many of Ma'am Jones' surviving sons as she could.

A forgotten facet of the family's history, however, is that they were among the first, or possibly THE first Anglo settlers in the vicinity of what would later become Roswell in the late 1860s. This is evidenced by correspondence between Roswell historian Maurice G. Fulton and Eve Ball when the latter was organizing her book. Fulton and Ball were going back and forth over the reliability of Ash Upson, the itinerant newspaperman and by default, an early-day historian, dubious though his claims sometimes were. Specifically, the topic of Upson's reliability in terms of the Joneses at Roswell came up.

North approach to bridge   *12-9-34*

The "North Bridge" of Missouri Plaza, the earliest known settlement of Chaves County where the Joneses were thought to have settled for a time. (HSSNM #1493D)

Mention the family tradition that Ash Upson was with [the Joneses] in 1866 but do not be too dogmatic about it. There was nothing in the Pecos Valley at that time except the Missouri Plaza settlement on the Hondo about 15 miles west of Roswell. Have you ever asked the Joneses if the family did not live for a time there? There were a few Mexican settlements down the Hondo all of which were "dried out".

Missouri Plaza, of which Fulton spoke, was a proto-settlement of Roswell defined by the presence of a large corral.[1] It was mostly populated by Spanish-Americans and immigrants from Mexico and was thought to have been deserted by 1871. According to Ball, Upson and the Joneses arrived in the vicinity of Missouri Plaza on July 4, 1866, possibly before the influx of Hispanic settlers.

An old dam   Missouri Plaza.   12-9-34

The "old dam" at Missouri Plaza. (HSSNM #1493F) Bill and Sam Jones, in a joint letter to Eve Ball, dated January 14, 1948, stated of the area: "When our family came [to Missouri Plaza] there was hardly anybody but Apaches and Mexicans. The Apaches surely had the Mexicans and Spaniards number; they did not fool much with the Apaches."

On a spot along the Hondo River, Upson suggested the Joneses may as well build a home there, which they did. Regarding their roof, he warned of heavy rains and advised them against planting too many of their seeds at once, as farming without irrigation in the area was nearly impossible due to droughts. Upson warned Mr. Jones to be cautious when killing a buffalo (of which there were actually none left in the area) and that he should be careful so as to avoid conflict with the Apaches. The family settled as Upson suggested, and while there, Thomas Edwin Jones was born on September 27, 1867, making him one of the first Anglo children to be born in the Roswell region.

This 1919 photograph shows eight of the surviving Jones children. In the back, from left to right, are Bruce (41), Henry (44), Nib (46), and Frank (47). In the front are Sam (49), Tom (52), Bill (57), and Jim (62). Missing are the deceased, John Jones, and Minnie Jones, the lone sister of the bunch. Courtesy Southeastern New Mexico Historical Society.

The Joneses didn't stay at Missouri Plaza for terribly long, though, and moved on. In addition to Ball, the same account of Missouri Plaza was more or less given to J. Evetts Haley by Bill Jones in a 1927 letter:

We came from Colorado, about Denver, down here. I was born within nine miles of Denver, and I am 63 years old. We first settled in the Missouri Plaza west of

46

Roswell on the Hondo, but the river failed and we went up further in the White Mountains, where we bought out three or four farms in there.[2]

Maurice Fulton exploring the remains of John Chisum's headquarters at the Bosque Grande where James Jones worked. (HSSNM #1440R)

This was corroborated in greater detail by Bill's older brother, James P. Jones, to Haley again in another 1927 letter. James's testimony was trustworthy as he was a young man who had worked for John Chisum at his Bosque Grande headquarters in 1872. When it came to the settling of the family in the Roswell region, he remembered, "We built some old picket houses right on the bank of the Hondo where Roswell now stands. This was in 1867." Notably, he made mention of the primarily Hispanic population of the settlement and emphasized that they were the only Anglo settlers at the time:

The old Missouri Plaza … was 18 miles up the Hondo. All who lived there were Mexicans. We were the first white family to come into this country. My father began farming at first. The next year he bought cattle, Texas cows, the best cows on earth. He bought 100 head to start with. We stayed there until '69, left, and bought a farm on the Ruidoso eighteen miles east of the White Mountains, in 1870.[3]

Eventually, and again under the advisement of Ash Upson, the Joneses would settle in the vicinity of Seven Rivers, where they built their beloved trading post. However, the Joneses weren't done with Roswell just yet. As stated previously, Roswell was begat by Van C. Smith, who had since departed. A local man, Marion Turner, filed on the land, taking over one of the buildings and leaving the other for Upson. Actually, many think that Turner purchased the land on the advisement of Upson, who told him that as the land was vacant, it could therefore be filed upon by anyone, and so he did.

Roswell's first store and post office c.1883, after the Jones had departed. (HSSNM #376B)

John Jones was a friend of Turner's and also wanted in on the trading post ownership, so Turner cut him a deal, creating the Turner & Jones store. (It should be noted that Heiskell Jones, the patriarch, also had part ownership of the trading post with John.) Under their management, the store consisted mostly of whiskey and ammunition. In her book, Ball noted that the Roswell trading post was less profitable for the Joneses than the one at Seven Rivers and that Heiskell spent much of his time freighting to Las Vegas, New Mexico, for mail and supplies.

James Jones remembered running the store to J. Evets Haley thusly: "We had a home [at Roswell] and a store. We made one ship to Las Vegas a year. We would take a big wagon and three or four yoke of steers and buy flour, coffee, sugar, and clothes. We bought our saddle blankets, but made our own ropes of rawhide, our bridles, grits, and quirts."[4] Sam Jones also spoke of the mail delivery in Roswell to Ball when she was interviewing him for *Ma'am Jones*. Sam said,

> Our house was close to where the depot was in Roswell. We got our mail from Las Vegas before the railroad come. A man carried it in a one-horse buckboard. There wasn't a post office between 300 miles... I saw that mail carried with a horse a swimmin' the Pecos – the mail carrier would be gone so long going there and coming back we'd forget what he looked like.[5]

Most of the time, John was the only Jones situated at the store. As this was during the Lincoln County War, John's presence there greatly concerned his mother. In her notes and proto-draft of *Ma'am Jones*, Ball had the titular character fretting over John away in Roswell as the conflict began to simmer: "But she wished John were at home rather than in Roswell, because there was always a possibility that neutrality might become impossible in this conflict as it had in the Horrell War on the Ruidoso years ago."[6]

Inevitably, and as Ma'am feared, John and several other of the Jones boys joined the fight. Despite being friends with Billy the Kid and having worked for Chisum from time to time, the brothers ended up siding with the Murphy-Dolan faction. This was primarily because Chisum had always been at odds with the Seven Rivers ranchers; thus, when the "Seven Rivers Warriors" rode out, they sided with Murphy. This culminated in the semi-decisive Five-Day Siege at Lincoln that more or less ended the war. As stated previously, it occurred in mid-July and concluded with the Murphy-Dolan faction winning with the assist of military troops from Fort Stanton. While Alexander McSween's group, including the Regulators, holed up in his luxurious home, it burnt to the ground on the fifth day when the "Dolanites" set fire to it.

James Jones remembered the events leading up to the Five-Day Siege to J. Evets Haley in a letter, stating, "I was at Roswell when it started. I went to Las Cruces, and when I came back the thing was in full bloom." James said that on his way back, he had run into Sheriff George Peppin to wrangle every man that he could to the cause in Seven Rivers, to which James eventually agreed. "Buck Powell, who belonged at Seven Rivers, was at Lincoln that day, so he and I hiked it after the boys. In a way, he deputized us. He wanted us to go down and bring all the men we could get to Roswell," James said.

Photograph with an 'X' purporting to show the location of the McSween Home. (Courtesy HSSNM #3509)

James did so and returned to Roswell with a dozen men. "We had been there about a week or more scouting around when the other side made their first move," he remembered. James set out with older brother John and his much younger brother Bill to take part in the siege. As friends, the Jones boys did their best not to shoot pal Billy the Kid and vice versa, but accidents happen. During the fight, Billy did shoot John Jones as it turned out, but it's long been debated if Billy purposely shot him in a benign area, or if Billy shot him by accident. As always, multiple versions and opinions exist.

Frank Jones remembered the Five-Day Siege and his brothers' involvement thusly:

Jake Owens always said Billy was afraid of John. They were good friends. But Billy shot him through the side and broke two ribs at Lincoln. John got off his horse when Billy came out of the McSween house and ran for the wall. They were not trying to hit him – I can remember the thirteen riders – I saw them come back to Roswell from Lincoln. We were living at Roswell. Bill, Jim, and John were in that bunch.[7]

Bill Jones gave this rendition:

I think Billy was the leader of the Chisum side; we were good friends but on opposite sides of the war. When he came out of that house John told him to run – told him to hit the brush and he could guard the back. And he did.[8]

Captain Lea's boarding house, which was located next to the Turner & Jones Trading Post. (HSSNM #1977)

During that frightful time, Ma'am Jones and the rest of the children finally journeyed to Roswell, feeling it was the safest place to be. Ma'am was shocked to find her old pal Ash Upson had deserted the trading post, his whereabouts unknown.[9] Ball implied in the finished book that Ma'am killed time cleaning out the trading post to keep her mind off of her sons being in danger, and she was probably right. Finally, on the sixth night, Ma'am heard hoofbeats in the distance and could finally see that her sons had survived the battle. In addition to being the end of the Lincoln County War, it also served as the end of the Jones's tenure in Roswell.

As Thomas Jones remembered it, "At the end of the Lincoln County War, in early summer of 1878, the Jones family sold their part of Roswell to Capt. J.C. Lee and moved to Seven Rivers." Though their time in Roswell was relatively brief, the Jones of Seven Rivers are certainly a part of the area's legacy.

Chapter Notes

[1] It is said that the stone blocks that comprised the corral were later taken into Roswell to build the stone fence around Cahoon park.

[2] Bill Jones to J. Evetts Haley January 13, 1927 [L. Tom Perry Special Collections, Harold B. Lee Library, Brigham Young University, Eve Ball Papers]

[3] James P. Jones to J. Evetts Haley, 1927 [L. Tom Perry Special Collections, Harold B. Lee Library, Brigham Young University, Eve Ball Papers]

[4] Ibid.

[5] L. Tom Perry Special Collections, Harold B. Lee Library, Brigham Young University, Eve Ball Papers. [MSS 3096 Folder 14]

[6] Ibid, Eve Ball's Early Notes for *Ma'am Jones of the Pecos*. [MSS 3096 Box 13 Folder 6]

[7] Ibid, Frank Jones to Eve Ball (January 10, 1948). [MSS 250 Box 14 Folder 1]

[8] Ibid, Bill Jones to Eve Ball and Fay Bonnell (March 21, 1949).

[9] To be thorough, and although in *Ma'am Jones of the Pecos*, Ball said that Ash was in Roswell drunk, notes and interviews imply that Ash was nowhere to be found at that time.

6.
PAT GARRETT &
THE STOLEN HORSES

In the 1930s, scores of what could be termed "survivors of the Wild West" were interviewed by the Federal Writer's Project. The stories collected during this era were often as confusing as they were enlightening. The problem was that many of the old-timers that were interviewed were so advanced in years that it was often difficult for them to recall exact dates and names in the stories they told. Worse yet, some of them told bald-faced lies, knowing full well they could get away with them. As it was, there was also a lack of good record-keeping in the Old West, making said stories even harder to authenticate.

However, the story to follow is not a tall tale or an exaggeration, though the date on which it took place is certainly debatable. It concerned an act of bravado on the part of Pat Garrett, which his biographer, Leon Metz, claimed was what helped get him elected sheriff in *Pat Garrett: The Story of a Western Lawman*. Per Metz, prior to Garrett's 1880 election, a party of Comanche absconded with a herd of horses from a ranch in the Roswell vicinity. A posse of men, including Garrett, set out to get them back. As they ventured northeast of Roswell, they found some of the horses already dead. The Comanche realized they had taken more animals than they could handle and decided to slaughter many of them. In all, they stabbed 27 horses in the neck, killing 14 in the process.

Postcard depicting Garrett on horseback.

The posse trailed the Comanche all the way to Mescalero Spring, east of Roswell, where it appeared they had watered briefly and moved on. However, it soon became apparent that the posse had not packed sufficient supplies to go any further. C.D. Bonney, one of the men in the party, later remembered, "We had brought no water or food, and had to turn back."[1]

When other men turned back on the hard trail, Garrett and a few others prevailed. A week later, Garrett and the few remaining men marched into Roswell with the horses that were still alive and a "sack full of moccasins"—implying Garrett had killed a good number of the Comanche.

In the words of C.D. Bonney:

> A party headed by Pat Garrett found some of the band [of Comanches], and horses, and brought back moccasins and things as evidence, we asked no questions those days – we knew better – but we surmised a great deal. Anyway no more horses were stolen. [2]

For some, this image labeled as "Pat Garrett Dam on the Hondo River" is a bit puzzling since no such place name officially exists on maps. However, thanks to *The Autobiography of E. D. Balcolm (1871 – 1967)*, the caption can be explained. On page 129 of his autobiography, Balcom wrote, "Pat Garrett's home was very close to where the Hondo dam was constructed. In order to protect his home, the canal being not more than 63 feet from where it passed his house, a bulkhead and access spillway were constructed just below the house so that the flow of water could be controlled whenever necessary. His house was a large structure constructed of adobe bricks and was very nice for those times. In order to give access to the back of his house there had been constructed a bridge about 20 feet wide and extending away from the house fully 50 feet."

As stated before, according to Metz, this daring act caught the attention of the Roswellites, then part of Lincoln County. This, in turn, helped Garrett to win the election for sheriff, among other things. However, it's more likely that this incident took place after Billy the Kid was dead, not before. In his footnotes, Metz cited an interview with C.D. Bonney by Georgia Redfield in the *El Paso Times* as the source. And while Bonney did tell Redfield the story, he didn't arrive in Roswell until 1881 himself, after Garrett was elected. If Bonney was relating a story that he had heard as opposed to having taken part in, this wouldn't be a problem. But, as it was, Bonney implied that he had himself been among the men hunting the horses who turned back. It's also possible due to the way in which Bonney worded it that he and Pat Garrett were part of different posses altogether, as he never specified that he was riding with Pat Garrett, only that Garrett was the one in charge of the party that did get the Comanche raiders and the horses.

It's possible that Metz found some additional sources that indicated Garrett's story did take place prior to his election as sheriff. Metz was not one to manipulate information, so it's likely he either had good reason to believe the incident occurred prior to the election or that Metz, in sifting through a deluge of sources, simply forgot that C.D. Bonney didn't arrive in Roswell until 1881.

Interestingly, Garrett's friend Ash Upson took part in a similar horse hunting party, or possibly the same hunt as Garrett's. In a letter that Upson wrote in November of 1879, he detailed how he was part of a riding party trailing some Mescalero Apache onto the Llano Estacado, on which resides Mescalero Spring, where Bonney and Garrett hunted the stolen horses. Upson stated that he and his group "killed four Indians, got back 13 head of horses they had stolen, took three head of theirs, two Indian saddles, three bridles they had stolen from Americans, moccasins, beads, medicine pouches..."[3]

This sounds very similar to Bonney's story of Garrett returning to town with a sack full of moccasins. Furthermore, historians have never been able to pinpoint Garrett and Upson's first meeting. Perhaps the hunt for the stolen horses was it? Notably, Bonney mentioned 27 horses in all, 14 of which died. Upson mentioned recovering 13 horses. Since 13+14=27, the accounts would seem to literally add up. It's also possible that C.D. Bonney was misremembering his own horse hunt with one Garrett took part in 1879, prior to Bonney's arrival in the region, and also confused the Comanche for Mescalero Apache many years later.

All that said, it seems more likely that the incident actually took place in 1882, well after Billy the Kid was dead. Redfield had written up a manuscript on interesting sites outside of Chaves County, one of which was Mescalero Spring. Her entry on it would seem to confirm that the Garrett story occurred in 1882, and it also upped the number of stolen horses to fifty in all:

Mescalero Spring
From the Caprock

Mescalero Spring. (HSSNM #1439A)

Mescalero Springs... was opened up as a campsite by Mescalero Indians in the buffalo hunting days. Later – sometime in the 70s – J.P. White made a cattle camp at the springs for the LFD cattle company. Cattle of this outfit grazed in the fine grass lands for hundreds of miles in all directions. This land is now all fenced in and several ranch homes have been established in the Mescalero Springs district. In 1882 a band of Comanches stole 50 horses from a corral in the Capitan Mountains and came out to Mescalero Springs. A party of men – among them C.D. Bonney – then Indian scout, now living in Roswell – went after them. When crowded by their pursuers the Indians stabbed 27 of the horses (14 died) watered at Mescalero Springs, and disappeared. A party headed by Pat Garrett found some of the band of Comanches and brought back moccasins and other things as evidence that they had been subdued. No more were stolen.

Another photograph of Mescalero Spring taken
on September 6, 1937. (HSSNM #1439B)

While it's fun to wonder whether Garrett and Upson met on the latter's 1879 horse hunt, it seems more likely that Garrett carried out this heroic effort after he was elected sheriff in the year 1882. However Garrett and Upson met, a long-lasting friendship was formed, and the duo would go on to write *The Authentic Life of Billy the Kid* together.

Chapter Notes

[1] Redfield, "C. D. Bonney--Old Timer," Library of Congress, Folklore Project, Life Histories, 1936-39 [MSS55715: BOX A719].
[2] Ibid.
[3] Ibid.

7.
BILLY THE KID IN
ROSWELL

Despite often visiting Roswell, Billy the Kid, arguably New Mexico's favorite son, doesn't have the presence there that he does in many other New Mexico towns. To thank for that may have been Captain Lea. According to area folklore, when the Kid was visiting Ash Upson over lunch in the summer of 1879, Upson made it a point to stop Captain Lea as he was leaving the store to introduce him to the Kid. The duo chatted about the aftermath of the Lincoln County War, but before the Kid left, Lea laid down the law to him. Elvis E. Fleming quoted from an old Georgia B. Redfield article in his book *Captain Joseph C. Lea* regarding the interaction between Lea and the Kid. In it, Lea told the Kid, "Bonney, if I ever catch you here in Roswell cutting up any of your capers, I'll take my Winchester and fill you full of holes."[1]

"All right, Cap'in. I promise I won't ever cut up any capers in your Roswell,"[2] the Kid was said to reply. However, this was probably a folktale related to Redfield.[3] That the Kid would be afraid of Lea seems unlikely, and perhaps he never caused any trouble in Roswell simply because he didn't want to. At the time, the Kid was developing a reputation as a cattle rustler and a bad man. Prior to this, in 1878, the Kid had also fallen in with a counterfeiting ring which was passing bad bills in Lincoln and White Oaks. Sent to investigate was Azariah F. Wild, an agent of the United States Treasury Department.

Surroundings of "Billy-the-Kid" Spring.   7-14-35

Billy had a notably hideout in present day Chaves County that eventually became known as Billy the Kid Springs. It's actually the only hideout of the Kid's that was officially named after him and recognized by the state. It is located on the San Juan Mesa, 14 miles northwest of Kenna. The locale consists of a concave which houses a spring beneath an overhang. Local lore states the spring is cool year-round as the sunlight never touches it. In the words of the write up, "The water is cool and good, a little gyp[sum]." About 100 yards from the spring are the ruins of a small dugout which "is supposed to be one of Billy the Kid's hideouts… the country is rough and broken. It is a very interesting place to see." It's entirely possible that the one place named for the Kid is a spot he never actually hid out in, either. (HSSNM #1489C & #1489E)

"Billy-the-Kid's" house   One of his hide-outs   7-14-35

In an interview with Georgia Redfield in April of 1937, May Corn Marley, daughter of Martin V. Corn, claimed that the horse the Kid escaped on from the Lincoln County courthouse in April of 1881 was raised by her father: "When my father and family came to New Mexico they brought three or four hundred head of cattle and a hundred head of horses. He loved horses. He raised the horse that Billy the Kid made his escape on, when he broke jail in Lincoln after killing Brady. It was a black horse. Pat Garrett bought him from my father and named him "Black Mart" after my father." Pictured above is "The Last Escape of Billy the Kid" by Roswell-born Peter Hurd.

Wild arrived in October of 1878 to begin his investigation and even went so far as to disguise himself as a dirty old miner during his undercover work. While a U.S. Marshall in the area was too afraid to assist Wild, Pat Garrett and a group of others, including Captain Lea, were willing, so Wild managed to make the men deputy U.S. Marshals. To that end, Garrett helped install a mole in Fort Sumner by the name of Barney Mason. The ploy worked, and Mason discovered that the money was likely coming from a mysterious, unnamed New York man. The outlaws who had been given the counterfeit bills were instructed to try and purchase $30,000 worth of Mexican cattle to be delivered to the Dan Dedrick ranch at Bosque Grande.

Rumor had it that the bills were being printed in an old cave somewhere near White Oaks. However, other tales placed it closer to Roswell in the vicinity of a place called Lost River. This is because in 1893, an old horse trough along with a coat was found in one of the Lost River caves. In the coat's pocket was said to be the bill of sale for several thousand head of cattle from a "former, long departed, cattleman." It was also said the cave was used by a counterfeiter ring long ago. There, in the darkness, they would make their counterfeit dollars. Could it have been the same counterfeiters in league with the Kid? It's possible.

According to the reminiscences many years later of Deputy J. Smith Lea in the *Roswell Daily Record* of May 3, 1930, Pat Garrett and his deputies purchased ammunition from C.D. Bonney before heading north to Fort Sumner the fateful day before Garrett gunned down the Kid. As such, that would mean that the bullet that killed the Kid came from Roswell. The store where he bought the bullets would have been the one initially operated by Van C. Smith, which by 1881 was jointly owned by Captain Lea and his newly arrived partner, C.D. Bonney.

While the tale of the Lost River counterfeiters is only rumor, for certain a posse including Wild, Garrett, Mason, and "Pecos Bob" Olinger departed Roswell heading north for Bosque Grande. On the trail, they arrested Texas outlaw Joseph Cook, who was rumored to be a part of the Kid's gang. Wild took him back to Roswell with several others to be held. When Wild and the lawmen left the small hamlet, the Roswellites were terrified as rumors floated that a gang of cutthroats planned to burn the town down and rescue Cook. So paranoid were the citizens that they barricaded themselves in the post office.

However, the story ended with a whimper rather than a bang. Roswell didn't burn to the ground, and no siege ever occurred. The only men Garrett and Wild managed to arrest in regard to the counterfeiter ring were John J. Webb and George Davis, who were only mildly involved in the scheme. The Kid and his gang had ridden away to steal and thieve another day, and from this point forward, Billy spent most of his time gambling and rustling cattle, notably from John Chisum, who the Kid felt owed him wages from the Lincoln County War during his service as a Regulator.

This is what led Chisum to campaign to get Pat Garrett elected as Sheriff, which he was on November 2, 1880. After this, the hunt for the Kid was on, culminating in his capture at Stinking Springs in December of 1880. The details of the Kid's infamous escape from the Lincoln County courthouse in April of 1881, a few weeks before his scheduled hanging, need not be recounted here. However, between his April escape and his July 1881 death at the hands of Garrett, the Kid's whereabouts were unknown. Papers of the day delighted in speculating on the Kid's activities at this time. One of these fictional exploits involved Roswell.

Prior to the apocryphal killing of the Chisum cowboys about to be recounted, Frank Jones told a tale wherein Billy avenged a dead cook on the Chisum range. (Although he didn't specify the date, this incident would have occurred before Billy was captured by Pat Garrett in late 1880.) According to Jones: "Billy started from Seven Rivers to Roswell and he found a chuckwagon with the tongue propped up at a high elevation. When Billy got there old Andy Boyle [the cook] was hanging from that wagon tongue. It had a gooseneck and a piece of iron ran through the tongue; a rope ran through that and the rope was around Andy's neck. He followed the murderers to seven miles this side of Chisum's old headquarters at South Springs River and killed these two men. Nobody ever knew their names or who they were." [Frank Jones to Eve Ball (January 10, 1948) MSS 3096 box 14.]

This apocrypha was thanks to the Las Vegas *Optic* running a story on June 10, 1881, that Billy approached a cow camp near Roswell and asked one of the hands, "Are you working for old John Chisum?" When the man affirmed that he was, the Kid quipped, "Well, here is your pay," and shot him dead. Then Billy turned his gun on the other three men and killed two. The third he let live and told him to deliver this message to Chisum: "Tell him during the Lincoln County War he promised to pay me $5 a day for fighting for him. I never got a cent. Now I intend to kill his men wherever I meet them, giving him credit for $5 every time I drop one." The article dramatically

2273 "Billy The Kid", New Mexico's Notorious Outlaw

concluded that "...at the rate he [the Kid] is now going, he will soon depopulate Lincoln County."

As some sources quote that Billy believed Chisum owed him $5,000; that would mean he would have to kill 1,000 men to get even! Of course, Chisum didn't even have 1,000 men under his employ. Still, many of the old-timers considered this story to be fact. One of them, Travis Windham, commented, "As an outgrowth of this, Billy the Kid did the one mean thing—the one thing and only thing that I really held against him. He killed two of Chisholm's [sic] riders who hadn't done a thing to him and in a cold-blooded manner. He did it as a warning to his employer."

If it actually happened, then it was one of the Kid's last acts of bravado and violence. Only a month after the story of the slain Chisum cowboys was printed in June, papers reported that the Boy Bandit King himself had been put down by Pat Garrett in Fort Sumner in mid-July. As a testament to his now legendary deed, a statue of Pat Garrett riding out of Roswell to kill the Kid stands behind the Chaves County courthouse today.

Chapter Notes

[1] Fleming, *Captain Joseph C. Lea*, p.82.
[2] Ibid.
[3] The story sounds suspiciously similar to one Deluvina Maxwell told J. Evetts Haley in 1927. In it, Billy and Pete Maxwell were having fun shooting at turkeys at Fort Sumner. Mrs. Maxwell came out and allegedly said, "Stop that shooting around here; I don't want to be scared to death." Billy was said to reply, "All right, Mother Maxwell, I won't shoot any more about here." It's likely that old timers liked to boast of people who could tame the Kid. A mothering figure like Mrs. Maxwell was probably more capable of that than Captain Lea.

8.
THE MAN WHO INVENTED
BILLY THE KID

Long before Walter Noble Burns arrived on the scene with his *Saga of Billy the Kid* in the 1920s, it was the largely fictitious events presented in Pat Garrett's book *The Authentic Life of Billy the Kid* that were "remembered" as fact by countless old timers who "knew" the Kid. However, many are unaware Garrett didn't even write the book, his friend Ash Upson did. Largely forgotten today, Upson was not only an important chronicler of Roswell's early history, he was also a colorful character and influential personality within the town.

Before settling in Roswell in the 1870s, if Upson's accounts are to be believed, he buddied around New York with Edgar Allen Poe, tutored the children of Mormon leader Brigham Young, was appointed Adjutant General of New Mexico Territory by Governor Robert Mitchell in 1869, and boarded in Silver City with Catherine Antrim and her two sons, one of whom would grow up to become Billy the Kid. Naturally, some doubt this claim, among them Upson's contemporary James M. Miller of Roswell, who once said, "Ash's report as being as one of the family with Billy's mother was all a frame up. He never saw the Kid until the Lincoln County War started."

Early-day Roswell chronicler and postmaster Ash Upson.

Whatever the case, Upson shared a few similarities with his literary creation "Billy, the Kid," whom Upson claimed was born on November 23, 1859, in New York, wandered West with his family, and eventually left home due to a difficult relationship with his step-father (well, that, and stabbing a man to death in Silver City). In fact, Marshal Ashmun Upson was himself born on November 23, 1828, in South Carolina. Though raised in Wolcott, Connecticut, Upson left home at a young age due to an argumentative relationship with his own father and drifted to New York where he eventually wrote for the New York *Herald*. Upson

Sketch of Upson, possibly by Lily Casey or Florence Muzzy.

spent his early days as a jour (or journeyman) writing for numerous newspapers such as the *Cincinnati Inquirer* and getting into various brawls. In 1862 his left eyebrow was split open, in 1864 his nose got smashed in at the "Dirty Woman's Ranche" in the Rockies and, in 1867, he was shot through the cheek and chest with a Smith & Wesson pocket pistol.

In 1866, he was found wandering outside of Denver, Colorado, by Heiskell and Barbara "Ma'am" Jones (it was their assumption he had been run out of town). It was Upson who then guided the couple and their brood down the Pecos to Seven Rivers as covered earlier. After drifting back to New Mexico, Upson began the Las Vegas *Mail*, which would eventually turn into the Las Vegas *Gazette* when it was purchased by Simeon Newman. In late 1871, Upson was the lone Anglo on a wagon trail to Fort Stanton, where he and his friend Calvin Simpson were to start a mercantile business. Instead, Simpson opened a bar, which Upson had no interest in running despite being a notorious alcoholic.

Upson's recollections of early-day Roswell were thankfully preserved by his niece, Florence Muzzy, pictured above. Courtesy Frank Abrams.

Upson next connected with Robert Casey and lived at his ranch where he became the area schoolteacher. "My pupils are all very good in behavior except for the larger growth," he wrote in a letter to relatives, referring to grown men, among them Lincoln Sheriff Ham Mills, "a six footer who has killed three men and innumerable Indians in his time." Among the children he taught was Lily Casey, who would grow up to fondly remember Upson in her classic autobiography *My Girlhood Among Outlaws*. She said of him, "A better teacher, I am sure, never lived."

Robert Casey was a political enemy of Lawrence G. Murphy, the big boss in Lincoln, and as a result found himself assassinated by William Wilson—a Murphy stooge. Upson was present for and wrote a newspaper account of the notorious "Double Hanging" of Wilson, who wasn't killed the first time he was strung from the gallows. This article was a precursor of things to come, for when Upson later found himself in Roswell surveying for John Chisum, he would become a war correspondent of sorts in the Lincoln County War.

During the war, Upson served as postmaster of Roswell, and actually managed to keep the peace there by threatening to shut the office down if violence occurred in his vicinity. As both sides needed their mail, this ploy worked, and the peace was kept in Roswell. Upson even ran a private mail service for Alexander McSween, whom he despised (Upson was, in fact, a closet Murphy-Dolan supporter).

At some unknown point in history, Upson met the new sheriff elect, Patrick F. Garrett. Though most assume Captain Lea introduced the duo, it's possible Upson was part of a riding party with Garrett, as discussed in a previous chapter. However they met, Upson and Garrett became fast friends, and after Garrett gunned down the Kid at Fort Sumner, he invited Upson to come and live at the Garrett ranch in August of 1881.

Pat Garrett, sitting on the far left, with other cowboys on the trail near Roswell. (HSSNM #566)

When Garrett became incensed at claims that he had killed the Kid unfairly, he partnered with Upson to write a book on the topic. The result was the notoriously mistitled *The Authentic Life of Billy the Kid*, rife with myths and tall tales. Since Upson knew the Kid in Roswell, and possibly in Silver City, why then did he make up elaborate fabrications about him? The answer is two-fold. For one, in 1882 many of the war's notorious bad men, be they political or otherwise, were still alive and writing about them in a negative light would have been dangerous. Perhaps more importantly though, Upson loved melodrama, and the book was his chance to write the great American novel. In a letter to his niece Florence Muzzy in 1870, he wrote, "There is no sense in reading novels, and yet I have neglected my meals to finish one."

Reportedly, he and Garrett argued about the book's tone, and Garrett lamented to his old deputy, James Brent, that he was greatly disappointed by the book's first draft. Though he tried to reign Upson in, he convinced Garrett the melodramatic tone would sell better. Unfortunately for Upson, Garrett in his characteristic poor business instincts, sold the book to Charles W. Greene, editor of the *Santa Fe New Mexican*. After the book's failure to sell many copies, Upson lamented to his sister in May of 1882 that

> [The book] has been bungled in the publication. The Santa Fe publishers took five months to do a month's job and then made a poor one. Pat F. Garrett, who killed the Kid, and whose name appears as the author of this work (although I wrote every word of it) as it would make it sell, insisted on taking it to Santa Fe, and was swindled badly in his contract.

Pat Garrett, pictured in front of his Roswell home with his wife and children. Upson also lived with them at the home for a time. (HSSNM #1887)

Ironically, in December of 1881 as Upson was working on the book, he took a trip to Toyah, Texas, with Charles Siringo, the famous Cowboy Detective. In Toyah, the two drunkenly rang in the New Year, but while on the trail Upson regaled him with his tales of Billy the Kid, which Siringo put into his own book, *A Texas Cowboy*, in 1885. The book became a bestseller, largely due to the Kid's inclusion, prompting Siringo to write future books heavily focused on the Kid, all utilizing Upson's stories from *Authentic Life*.

Despite the book's failure, Upson had dreams of writing a follow-up on the Lincoln County War, one which would presumably go to a publisher back east as he had wished *Authentic Life* would. Supposedly, Upson kept these writings in a small trunk he carried with him everywhere up until his death. His demise occurred in Uvalde, Texas, where he had moved with Garrett in 1892. In 1893, Upson took a trip to visit his dying mother back east, and along the way got into a few drunken "tares" and even ended up in jail. When he failed to return to Uvalde, the *Roswell Register* fantastically reported, "It is feared that he now lies in an unknown grave, in a strange land and that his fate may never be known." Upson would have surely been pleased at the sensational attention he received.

However, Upson didn't last long once he returned to Uvalde, as he had contracted influenza. On October 6, 1894, he passed away at the Garrett Ranch. On November 3rd Garrett wrote to Upson's sister, "We buried him in the city grounds at my expense. He has a trunk here and clothing. What shall I do with them?"

The trunk Garrett spoke of was likely the one that contained Upson's book on the Lincoln County War. Unfortunately, to this day the mysterious trunk has never been found. What elaborations, fallacies, and perhaps even truths it contained will unfortunately never be known.

Thomas B. Catron when he served as a U.S. Senator.

9.
ROSWELL AND THE SANTA FE RING

Although Roswell was able to remain neutral during the infamous Lincoln County War, the little village had some rather interesting ties to the villains of the war, that being the Santa Fe Ring. Though thought of as a secret society, the Santa Fe Ring was less of an Illuminati-like organization and simply a like-minded group of Republican politicians. Through political corruption and fraudulent land deals they amassed a fortune in the late 19th and early 20th centuries.[1] For the most part, Lawrence G. Murphy, the main bad guy of the Lincoln County War, was considered to be a member of the Santa Fe Ring, while John Chisum, Alexander McSween, and John Tunstall were not.

The leader of the Santa Fe Ring was usually identified as Thomas B. Catron, a powerful U.S. Attorney for New Mexico in 1878 during the Lincoln County War. Pertaining to Roswell, it's interesting to note that Catron was said to be a friend of Van C. Smith. Many sources even attest that it was Catron who suggested that Smith buy James Patterson's trading post along the Rio Hondo. Later, Chaves County was itself named for a prominent member of the Santa Fe Ring.[2] Add to this the fact that a small settlement northeast of Roswell was named for another ring-member, Stephen B. Elkins, and it's apparent that Chaves County has many interesting connections to the nefarious ring.

Back to the origins of Roswell; although Van Smith may have owned the trading post and post office for a time, John Chisum was still the "big boss" of the area. As one of the wealthiest men in the territory and as an opponent of the Santa Fe Ring, he faced off against Catron in court several times. Some have theorized Catron wanted to see Chisum done away with to take away his range claims. Chisum was even arrested in Las Vegas, New Mexico, on his way to Colorado on Christmas Eve of 1877. This was done because, at the time, Chisum was trying to take control of Van Smith's old property. The true ownership of the land that the trading post sat upon had been somewhat nebulous since Smith had it deemed an official post office in 1873.

In the words of Ash Upson, "The smash came in 1873, and T.B. Catron and L.G. Murphy held mortgages which covered all the property possessed by Smith..."[3] In his history of Van Smith, Frederick Nolan clarified that by the end of 1876, Smith had lost his foothold on Roswell. As such, on January 5, 1877, Roswell Smith, acting under power of attorney from his son, "executed a mortgage to Thomas B. Catron on property within the present city of Roswell to secure a loan of $1000."[4]

Likewise, in his book *Thomas Benton Catron and His Era*, author Victor Westphall stated that on September 24, 1877, Smith had conveyed his property to Catron by warranty deed. "This land gave Catron headquarters for the cattle received from [James] Dolan [partner of Lawrence Murphy] and [John] Riley," Westphall wrote.

The little settlement of Elkins in Chaves County was named after politician Stephen B. Elkins, who was considered to be the second most powerful man in the Santa Fe Ring after his friend, Thomas B. Catron. The post office at Elkins was established on April 20, 1907. Above is pictured the Frank Carroll store in Elkins c.1917. (HSSNM #4133)

Frederick Nolan continued that when John Chisum discovered that Smith's rights to the property were "imperfect," Chisum "obstructed the purchase" by having Marion Turner file a formal claim on the land. Nolan speculated, "Whether this was random pique or whether Chisum was acting to prevent a larger plan by the Santa Fe Ring to gobble up the town site is not clear, but if the latter it certainly succeeded."[5] Turner, in turn, sold his 160 acres on August 1, 1878, after the Lincoln County War had ended, to Captain Joseph C. Lea, another ally of Chisum's.

Interestingly, though not a ring supporter, later Lea would end up naming Chaves County after one of the big bosses of the Santa Fe Ring: Colonel J. Francisco Chaves. Actually, to say Chaves was one of the big bosses of the ring might be an embellishment, but he was certainly a powerful man in New Mexico and definitely in league with the ring. In an entry on Chaves from *Hispanic Americans in Congress*, it was stated, "[Chaves] became a powerful political player through his interaction with the Santa Fe Ring, a group composed mainly of republican lawyers and business professionals who dominated New Mexican politics. A number of sources alleged that Chaves controlled a political machine out of Valencia County."[6]

Chaves County's namesake, Colonel J. Francisco Chaves.

Chaves came from a prominent family and was the grandson of Francisco Xavier Chaves, first governor of New Mexico Territory when it was under Mexican rule in 1822. Chaves did a great deal for the territory, serving often in the territorial House of Representatives. Chaves presided over the 1889 constitutional convention, hence why Captain Lea promised to name the new county after him if he voted in favor of it, which he did.

It's possible that Colonel Chaves's association with the Santa Fe Ring got him killed. In 1904, he had just finished acting as the Superintendent of Public Instruction and had been commissioned as the first state historian. Chaves was hard at work writing a book on the history of New Mexico, which no one was ever able to see. Chaves was eating dinner inside of his home at Pinos Wells in Torrance County on November 26, 1904, when an assassin's bullet sailed through his glass window, killing him almost instantly. Chaves's funeral was the largest ever attended in Santa Fe up until that time.

Though a cattle rustler named Domingo Valles was arrested under suspicion of firing the fatal shot, it could never be proved that he had done so. Others felt the assassination was politically motivated. Marc Simmons told Don Bullis in *Unsolved: New Mexico's American Valley Ranch Murders & Other Mysteries* that he had talked to "an old-timer living near Chaves' birthplace" who told him that he met the real killer in 1950 when the man was on his deathbed. According to Simmons' source, the killer claimed that he had been paid by "certain unscrupulous politicians" to carry out the "terrible act."[7]

If these "unscrupulous politicians" were allies or enemies of the Santa Fe Ring is unknown, as were their exact reasons for wanting Colonel Chaves dead.

Chapter Notes

[1] Furthermore, it's unknown if the group actually called themselves the Santa Fe Ring and, in fact, it was a name bestowed upon the cabal by the press and New Mexico residents.

[2] Some have erroneously claimed that Chavez was deliberately misspelled as Chaves to "please a bunch of Texans living [in Roswell] at the time; people who did not approve of naming the county for an Hispanic..." [Bullis, *Unsolved*, p.54]

[3] Upson, "Roswell: Something Its Past History," *Roswell Record* (April 08, 1892).

[4] Nolan, "Van C. Smith," *New Mexico Historical Review* (April 1997), p.24.

[5] Ibid.

[6] *Hispanic Americans in Congress*, p.113.

[7] Bullis, *Unsolved*, p.57.

Bottomless Lake.

Bottomless lakes, mysterious,
rugged mountains in the West
all gold in the evening's glow,
when the sun sinks to rest.
Crystal clear waters, deep, cold,
Strung 'round foothills' crest —
cradled in their rocky bowl
asleep, the world at rest.
Waters sparkling like gems
in the last sunset raise,
weird silence, all, peace
while souls lift in praise.
—Georgia Redfield

10.
BOTTOMLESS
LAKES

Before UFOs, Roswell mainly promoted Bottomless Lakes State Park, located 12 miles east of town, as its main tourist draw. Nearly any publication geared towards drawing visitors to the Pecos Valley heavily promoted Bottomless Lakes as a true wonder of the Southwest. The publicity wasn't unwarranted though; the lakes are quite an anomaly in the arid deserts of Southeastern New Mexico. Georgia Redfield, for instance, described them as being "unique in freakish beauty."

An old promotional magazine, *The Roswell Way*, touted the lake's beauty in nearly every issue they published. This description is worth reprinting in full:

> [The] bluffs [of Bottomless Lakes] themselves are of genuine interest. Touched with enough mica to make them sparkle in the sunlight, their peculiar coloring changes under different light conditions. Early in the morning they present one effect – later in the day another – and still later a different appearance. The next day – perhaps – you will find an entirely different combination of colors – due to clouds, or atmosphere not quite as clear as the day before.

Chaves County residents can take pride in the fact that Bottomless Lakes was actually the very first state park to be sanctioned in New Mexico in 1933 by the Civilian Conservation Corps. Eight of the nine "bottomless" lakes, in actuality sinkholes ranging from 17 to 90 feet in depth, comprise Bottomless Lakes State Park, encompassing 1,611 acres open to the public. Hiking trails are available throughout the park, swimming and scuba diving are allowed in the clear waters of Lea Lake, and fishing is allowed in several others stocked with catfish and rainbow trout as long as one has a license.

As stated before, eight lakes make up the park, and *The Roswell Way* of February 15, 1921, described the lakes individually as follows:

There are eight lakes in the group following the line of the bluffs, named beginning with the one farthest south: Dimmitt Lake, named for L.W. Dimmitt of Roswell who homesteaded the land upon which the lake is situated back in 1883; Lea Lake, named for Joseph Lea, one of the famous pioneers of this district; Canvasback Lake, so-called from the fact that the ducks of that variety seem to show partiality for this particular lake; Figure Eight Lake, named for its peculiar shape; the Devil's Inkwell, thus named because of its resemblance to an inkwell or a jug; Pasture Lake, so called because it formerly lay in a pasture Jaffa Prager Co. had fenced in for sheep, sometimes called "Freak Lake," because tradition has it that ducks have a particular aversion to alighting on it; Cottonwood or Tree Lake, named from the solitary cottonwood which stands on its banks;[1] and Sutherland Lake, named for Dr. Sutherland, the first doctor in this part of the country, who built his house on the shore of the lake about 1880.[2]

Speaking of Dr. Sutherland, the discovery of the lakes were fairly cryptic thanks to him. This is because he had in his possession a manuscript pertaining to the finding of the lakes which he would never let anyone else see. Lacking the mysterious manuscript, what we do know is that the lakes were first discovered in the 1840s by an old Indian fighter from Texas named Gabriel Thompson.

Thompson was chasing some Apache toward the mountains when he came across the lakes. Although he was barely literate, Thompson wrote an account of his adventure, which years later Dr. Sutherland somehow acquired. What mysteries, if any, the document held can only be speculated upon since "It was one of the peculiarities of Dr. Sutherland that he didn't trust anybody, and all efforts to get access to the story of the hunter proved unavailing," wrote Will Robinson back in 1948 for an article in *The Roswell Morning Dispatch*.

The lakes would further puzzle cowboys traveling the Goodnight-Loving Trail when they attempted to determine the depths of the lakes. Tying rocks to their lariats, the cowhands threw them in the lake, and when one would not reach the bottom they would tie another and then another and so on, never finding the bottom. Hence the sinkholes were named Bottomless Lakes. What the men did not realize, however, was that the lakes were not bottomless; their lariats had simply been swept away by underwater currents.

Actually, the cowboy rumored to have named the lakes was Billy the Kid himself. James M. Miller wrote in *Reminiscences of Roswell Pioneers* how he came across Billy the Kid at John Chisum's commissary at South Springs while he was there to get supplies. According to Miller, this occurred just a few days after Billy's famous April 1, 1878, killing of Sheriff William Brady in Lincoln. Miller said the Kid was sitting on the counter when he told him the tale of the mysterious Bottomless Lakes, where he and his pals had a hideout they used.

"The Skillet" as it was called in this photograph, was reputed to be an old hideout of Billy the Kid's in the Bottomless Lakes area. (HSSNM #3415)

Regarding he and the Kid's conversation, Miller wrote:

I heard him say something about the Bottomless Lakes, as a natural curiosity not far from the cave in which Billy and his pals were hiding. As I was a newcomer and did not know about the lakes, I asked why they were called 'bottomless'? Billy answered pleasantly enough and explained that not long before, at a big round-up [for Chisum], he and some other 'boys' had tied together all of their picket ropes, and had tried to find out the depth of two of them, without being able to reach the bottom. Then he added (I remember his very words) 'There is fish in them lakes as black as my hat,' pointing to the broad-brim felt hat he was wearing.[3]

Historians have concurred that while Miller likely had his dates mixed up on when exactly he encountered the Kid, it is likely that the Kid came across the lakes while working for Chisum.[4] Per the words of old-timer Nib Jones to Eve Ball, "[Chisum] owned Bottomless Lakes on the Pecos, East of Roswell..."[5] (But then again, back then, Chisum unofficially owned just about all the land between current-day Carlsbad and Fort Sumner.)

Mirror Lake. (HSSNM #293B)

That Billy may have helped name the lakes is now part of their folklore. However, the Bottomless Lakes area is rich in myth and legend outside of the Kid's involvement. One of the earliest tall tales told by the old-timers was that a horse that drowned in one of the Figure Eight lakes (the two adjoining lakes that form a figure eight) later bobbed to the surface of the adjoining lake. Another told of an old Mexican sheepherder with failing eyesight who followed his flock of sheep, who were jumping into the lake one after the other, to their doom and they all sunk down "clear to China."

Like so many others, that folktale was unearthed by Georgia Redfield. One night, Redfield and a group of friends were visiting the lakes when they came across an old timer who told them the tale. In her write-up, "The Legends of the Lakes," Redfield gave the following rendition:

Then there is the legend of the old sheepherder and the lost sheep, best told as related to the writer, in the words of a man discovered tossing stones into the water and watching as they slowly disappeared without hitting bottom:

"Gosh!" the man exclaimed, "It's gone clean down to China! Just like the lost flock. You see this here big rock what I'm a-settin' on? You'd be surprised if I'd tell you it's a tombstone, wouldn't you? Well, that's just what it is—a tombstone of a silly ol' sheepherder... the leader of a whole flock of silly sheep that smelled water, when they was all parched out and dry, and jumped over that their precipice one by one, right into the deep water of this here lake. Then the old half-blind sheepherder comes along, and he jumps right in after them, and they all sinks plum outs o' sight, right there under that big tall cliff over there.

He digressed to the beginning of the story and explained that the old shepherd had "started out that morning to move the flock o' sheep to new pastures, cause all the water and grass had dried up on the old pasture." Along with the sheepherder was his little grandson, who survived to tell the story. The little boy had "sat down to res' a minute in the shade of some rocks over in them bluffs."

The old-timer continued,

> He was all tuckered out and the sheep was too. It was a
> hot blisterin' day in July. The sheep was jus' a pantin' and
> a bleatin'—almo' dead for water when the little Mexican
> boy got up an' started to drive 'em on again. All to once
> the ol' sheep leader scented water an' he started on a run
> and the rest of 'em followed and they all rushed past the
> boy, and went headlong right square over this here ledge,
> into that deep water right down there. [6]

Redfield wrote, "The man paused for breath a moment and
seeing eager interest in our faces, started again on his amazing
story" continuing that the little boy watched helplessly as his
half-blind grandpa tumbled over the bluff with the sheep. "He
looked and looked down on the water but they never been
found to this day," the old-timer stated bluntly. Then he
pointed to the edge of the bluff and said, "You see the high
stone arch what looks like a pile of rocks just over there a
piece?"

One of Redfield's friends answered that it looked like a stone
bridge. The old-timer replied, "Well, sir, that's just what it is.
It's what you call a natural bridge. Well, them sheep just went
on down under this big rock" and got pulled "into a running
stream underneath here. Listen can you hear it?"

In Redfield's own words,

> We heard absolutely nothing. There was the deep quiet
> and hush that always comes to this place after the sunset
> hour. It was growing late. The lakes looked weird and
> mysterious – creepy looking. We walked on down to the
> natural bridge which was the dividing line between two
> of the deep lakes. Our newly made friend continued his
> story.
>
> "Yessir, the whole flock of sheep an' the old herder
> swept right on down the river which is a' runin' under
> where we were standing an' comes out through here and
> under that there natural bridge, and was carried on under
> them big rocks out of sight.

Now, all them sheep done multiplied tills they's the biggest flock you ever heard of, and the little lambs frolic in the new green pastures they started out to find. You can hear them playing on bleak nights, when it's still and quiet.

He turned unexpectedly when he heard a whispered remark of one of our crowd. "So, you think I'm touched in the head, do you?" he asked. "Well, maybe I am."[7]

Postcard of Lea Lake.

More modern folklore likes to contend that the lakes are somehow connected to Carlsbad Caverns via underwater currents. One wild rumor even alleged that a missing car that sunk in the lakes resurfaced in the caverns. However, a car turning up in Carlsbad Caverns would have made the national news, if such a thing was even possible. But it does make for a wonderful modern-day folk tale.

And, while the lakes may not really be "bottomless," the fact that so many early-day residents thought that they were has made them rather endearing. According to an old issue of *The Roswell Way*, during the establishment of Bottomless Lakes State Park, state officials suggested a "better permanent name" for the park. However, this resulted in "a loud protest from old-timers and the younger generation," which "quickly stopped that discussion."

We're glad that it did.

Chapter Notes

[1] It was apparently eventually torn down per Georgia Redfield, who noted how Cottonwood Lake was named for "a loan cottonwood tree, a landmark in the area for many years, until it was ruthlessly cut down."

[2] Also listed was a ninth unofficial lake, "Shallow Lake "which properly is not included in the bottomless group– just a few feet deep."

[3] Shinkle, *Reminiscences of Roswell Pioneers*, p.40.

[4] Billy was at Blazer's Mill in Mescalero after the Brady killing, not Chisum's commissary.

[5] Nib Jones to Eve Ball. [MSS 3096 Box 14 Folder 2]

[6] Redfield, "Tall Tale of the Lost Sheep," *Roswell Daily Record* (undated clipping in HSSNM Archives).

[7] Ibid.

Lover's Lane, east of Roswell. (HSSNM Larkham Album One, #822)

11.
LEGEND & LORE OF
LOVER'S LANE

Long before teenagers parked their cars at places like "Make-Out Point," young people in horses and buggies used to ride through the tree-strewn Lovers Lane east of Roswell. And instead of a hook-handed man, they had a headless horsewoman to terrorize them. But, before we get to the ghost, first, the origins of Lover's Lane itself. The mile-long area had its roots in an agreement between John Chisum and Martin V. Corn, a prominent early homesteader of the region. Corn and Chisum always had a strong relationship, and it was said that Corn's cattle ranged with Chisum's free of charge.

May Corn Marley, when being interviewed by Georgia B. Redfield on April 17, 1937, probably gave the best history of the origin of Lover's Lane:

> Soon after my father [Martin Corn] settled at the old home site of the Corn family south of Lover's Lane, John Chisum came to him one day and said, "Corn, I'll make you a proposition. If you set out trees here along this ditch, I'll get the trees. We need trees, lots of 'em on this hot, dry prairie."
>
> My father said he would plant them and care for them so Chisum sent two ox wagons to Alpine, Texas, in the Davis Mountains and got the cottonwood and willow trees. They grew fast and soon made the beautiful lane which has been a favorite drive for young people, especially lovers, for nearly sixty years.

Another child of Martin Corn told historian James Shinkle, "My father's place was the farm that joins what is known as Lover's Lane, on the south side; and I assisted [my father] when he took the cottonwood sticks, some twenty-four-inches-long and stuck them in the wet soil along the ditch..."[1]

For the entirety of its lifetime, the south side of the lane belonged to the Corn family, while the north side at first belonged to a man named Oregon Bell, who later sold to John W. Poe, who famously served as Pat Garrett's deputy the night Billy the Kid was shot.

Lover's Lane. (HSSNM #875B)

Lover's Lane was a cattle thoroughfare for many cattlemen, among them J.P. White. May Corn Marley said, "J.P. White told me just before he died that every time he started to drive cattle through that lane my father would say, 'Be sure to keep the cattle from destroying any of those trees, White.'"

"Mr. White said he would always promise to watch them and all of the thousands of cattle he drove through the lane, not one ever touched those trees that my father and John Chisum loved and tended so carefully," Marley concluded.

Nib Jones had fond memories of Lovers Lane on cattle drives, too, and remembered once when Sallie Chisum tended to his wounded eye.

> In '93 I got something in my eye. We were delivering a herd of cattle at the mouth of Lovers Lane, and Sallie Chisum was there. She cracked an egg, and she laid my head in her lap and she had some flax seed there in a bottle and she put some of them in my eye. That was the last time I ever saw Sallie.

The Headless Horsewoman of Lover's Lane by Neil Riebe.

When cattle weren't being driven through the tree-lined grove, it was a favorite spot for husbands and wives, and also younger couples in the process of courting, to go for a romantic, scenic drive. And naturally, a ghost was eventually conjured to scare the young lovers. According to an old issue of *Vision Magazine*, "100 years ago on nights when the moon was full and the wind was whispering through the branches of the cottonwood and willow trees, the headless horsewoman was said to appear on 'Lovers Lane' pining for her lost sweetheart."

A young woman, Adrian Gronsky, poses with a rifle in Lover's Lane during the winter when the trees were bare of leaves. The image is just coincidental and has nothing to do with the story of the "Headless Horsewoman of Lover's Lane." (HSSNM Larkham Album One, #774)

As the monstrous monicker suggested, she appeared as a woman dressed in white riding atop a horse, only she had no head. The story went that she had been the daughter of a wealthy banker set to marry a local man, until he left her for another woman. What made it even more humiliating was that he deserted her on their wedding day, leaving her at the church alone. One night the woman, in her wedding dress, came into her ex-fiancé's home and killed he and his new wife with a shotgun. After it was over, she turned the barrel on herself, the shotgun blast severed her head from her body, and from then on, her ghostly form terrified young couples along Lover's Lane. Like the water-based La Llorona, the headless horsewoman mainly stuck to an old iron bridge located in the middle of the road near Lover's Lane. There, she would wait atop her horse, ready to terrorize anyone who parked along the shady grove. However, when the bridge was washed out and replaced by a large sinkhole, the toppled bridge was shipped off and sold to Lincoln County. After this, sightings of the headless horsewoman dwindled until they turned into nothingness.

Sadly, along with the ghost, Lover's Lane itself faded away after about sixty years. In James Shinkle's *Martin V. Corn* booklet, a descendant stated that "the gigantic trees that form this lane have been topped, many of them cut away to make room and to use for fuel."[2] Robert F. Corn likewise stated to *Vision Magazine* that "the trees had become old and were a hazard" and so were cut down by the German POWs that were housed at Orchard Park in the 1940s.

Though long gone by anyone who can still remember it firsthand, Lover's Lane remains a legacy of Chaves County.

Chapter Notes

[1] Shinkle, *Martin V. Corn*, p.26.
[2] Ibid.

The Lost River outside of Roswell. (HSSNM Larkham Album Three)

12.
LORIUS LAKE
& THE MISSING MOTORISTS

During the mid-1930s, Chaves County was the site of a manhunt. On May 22, 1935, two couples from Illinois, Mr. and Mrs. George Lorius and Mr. and Mrs. Albert Herberer, disappeared while traveling through New Mexico in their automobile. Apparently they were last seen in Vaughn before they seemingly dropped off the face of the earth. An anonymous tip claimed the couple's car crashed into a lake in the vicinity of Bitter Lakes Refuge, and so one of the lakes was dragged in search of the bodies and the vehicle.

Located nine miles northeast of Roswell and about five miles north of the old Clovis Highway, before it became Bitter Lakes, it was originally called Lost River. It was so named because most of the river flowed underground, linking through a series of caves and grottoes. In the 1930s, Georgia B. Redfield said that if one wanted to experience "downright, flesh creeping spookiness, especially on a dismal rainy late evening" then they should visit "Desolate Lost River" and its "dangerous looking, caving, dead river banks," which cut "a zigzag course east through the most weird, deserted section of country in southeastern New Mexico."

As to how the place was ever discovered, supposedly an old Hispanic sheepherder was digging a well in the area of Lost River when he fell into an underground lake. Redfield wrote, "After his morning's work…he climbed out of the ten foot opening he had made, ate his lunch, then jumped back into the well to resume his digging, and dropped twenty feet into a lake below. He was almost paralyzed from fright, but seeing light in the distance he began swimming and wading through shallow water until he reached safety on the banks of Lost River, half a mile below the pool, or lake, into which he had dropped."[1]

While the area served as an interesting curiosity like Bottomless Lakes for a while, eventually the county deemed it too dangerous. In 1924, a man and woman parked their automobile on a riverbank and then walked down below to look at the river. The car collapsed the bank above them, crushing the couple to death. After the 1924 cave collapse, Lost River's crumbling banks were dynamited to prevent further tragedies. This brings us back to the summer of 1935, when one of the lakes within Bitter Lakes was searched for the missing motorists.

Redfield wrote,

> Since a recent visit to the isolated gypsum hills and alkali flats region of the lake, and gazing into the mysterious depths of the quiet waters, it is not surprising that credence was placed in the report to police by an unnamed person that the bodies of the tourists, believed to have been murdered, could be found, probably weighted down on the rocky bottom of the isolated lake.

A deep-sea diver out of Houston, Texas, was hired to scour the lake bottom, looking in every crevice. Though no bodies were found, one interesting discovery was made: "A missing touring car, however, on which insurance had been collected, was found (with tires still inflated) and was raised to the surface."[2] Stranger yet, it was later learned this car did not belong to Mr. Lorius, for his car was found sometime later in Dallas.

On June 29, 1935, two Albuquerque cowboys out riding their cattle range actually came across the couple's burned luggage and alerted the authorities. This led to the police following a trail of forged travelers checks belonging to Mr. Lorius all the way into Texas, hence the car being discovered in Dallas. As to the alleged murderer, there had been a man with a tattoo on one arm last seen driving the car, but he was never caught.

"SEEK BODIES OF VANISHED TOURISTS IN DESERT LAKE: Diving operations are shown here are being conducted in one of the Bottomless Lakes in the desert near Roswell, N.M. In an effort to find a key to the mystery that has defied solution for more than a year." (AP News Photo dated June 15, 1936.)

So, was the search at Lost River just a wild goose chase? Perhaps not. Later, a second tip, this time from an unidentified man from a penitentiary, said that the couples' bodies could be found northeast of Roswell in the vicinity of Bitter Lakes. Likewise, Redfield speculated that the "bodies of the unfortunate victims may have been weighted and wedged under, or between, huge boulders, fathoms deep under the still waters, where they could probably never be found." In any case, the lake was henceforth known as Lorius Lake, regardless of whether the bodies resided there or not.

Chapter Notes

---

[1] Redfield, "Yesterday and Today," (undated newspaper clipping).
[2] Ibid.

The Oasis Well as depicted on an old postcard. (HSSNM #32A)

13.
LA LLORONA
AT THE OASIS RANCH

Though it may seem hard to believe in today's arid climate, Roswell used to be regarded as a city that literally overflowed with water. This was, of course, largely thanks to the artesian wells of the late nineteenth and early twentieth centuries. Nowhere was this more apparent than at the Oasis Ranch, which boasted the biggest Artesian Well in the world for a time.

The Oasis Ranch was located within East Grand Plains just west of the Pecos River. In the words of lifelong resident and area historian Morgan Nelson, while the Oasis Ranch was certainly "a part of East Grand Plains... due to its size, it has been more isolated and independent from the rest of the community."[1] The first settlers in the area were Mormons in the spring of 1877. A bit later, James M. Miller, a prominent Roswell sheepman, oversaw what would eventually become the Oasis Ranch in the days of John Chisum, though it was more famously taken over by the Clardy family.

The record-breaking well was drilled in 1931 by Myron Bruning, a professional driller, who considered it his crowning achievement. According to Morgan Nelson, it was drilled "to a depth of 840 feet and flowed 9100 gallons per minute under a natural pressure of 32 pounds per square inch. When fully opened it would spout a pillar of water 7 feet above the 13-inch casing."[2]

Spectators watch as the Oasis Well gushes. (HSSNM #2807A)

Per a *New Mexico Magazine* article published in the August 1966 issue, the Oasis Well was "believed by many hydrologists to be the greatest freshwater artesian well in world history." It went on to report that in 1902, the *Roswell Record* could find no equivalents to the Oasis Well when compared to the artesian belts located in California, Illinois, Argentina and even Russia. In the *New Mexico Magazine* article, author Bob Koonce described the Oasis Well as "a symbol of hope for the Pecos Valley underground basin, probably the finest aquifer ever developed on earth."[3]

A neglected aspect of the Oasis Well's lore is that it was one of the main haunts of La Llorona in Chaves County. As we all know, the Wailing Woman is seen everywhere in New Mexico, and in the Roswell region, the Oasis Ranch was subject to her spectral wanderings. For their book *The Weeping Woman: Encounters with La Llorona*, authors Edward Garcia Kraul and Judith Beatty wrangled quite a few wailing woman stories from all over the Land of Enchantment. As to be expected, most of the tales came from northern New Mexico. However, via a witness identified as Isidro Guerrero, tales of La Llorona on the Oasis Ranch came to light.

Throughout the 1940s and 1950s, Guerrero's uncle was a field foreman at the Oasis Ranch. He told young Guerrero how La Llorona came from the Hondo Valley into Roswell and onto the Oasis Ranch from time to time. Specifically, Guerrero remembered that:

La Llorona was supposed to have appeared on several occasions at the south end of the ranch in an area full of big cottonwood trees – what we called *alamos*— where the irrigation ditches were. When there was such a sighting, word would spread quickly throughout the *campo*. She'd float among the trees in the dusk wearing a white cloak, moaning and screaming and scaring everybody half out of their minds.[4]

Guerrero heard most of these tales in 1943 when he was seven years old. At the age of 15, he was tasked by his uncle with irrigating the south end of the Oasis Ranch, which was exactly where the specter often appeared. Worse yet, he would have to do it at night. He recounted in the book how his best friend joked that he should take a crucifix with him to flash in the ghost's face lest she appear. However, Guerrero was too busy mending a busted ditch that overflowed into a cotton field that first night. "I spent the whole night shoveling in a high wind and trying to secure the ditch caps, and I forgot all about La Llorona," he remembered.[5] When his uncle asked if he had seen the ghost the next morning, he told him he didn't think so. In summing up his encounter to the authors, Guerrero said, "Later on, though, I thought to myself that maybe she had appeared by one of the trees and watched me work through the night. Could it have been La Llorona who made it such a difficult night for me?"[6]

The Oasis when it operated as the Clifton Chisolm Alfalfa Farm. (HSSNM #953)

Guerrero's tales of La Llorona at the Oasis Ranch in the 1950s occurred at the tail end of the Oasis Well's glory days, as it turned out. According to Nelson, "The big well stopped flowing completely in the summer of 1960 and a pump had to be put on it."[7] Prior to that, Mr. Clardy had given the area around the big well to the Girl Scouts to be used for summer camping, which was called the Clardy Day Camp. If the Girl Scouts ever ran into La Llorona there is unknown, as no stories have yet to surface. Interestingly, though, in an old historical address given to the Girl Scouts, the speaker claimed that when drilling the Oasis Well, the ranch manager had instructed Myron Bruning to "drill a well to the 'Devil's Domain' if necessary to find plentiful water."[8] If they did indeed tap into the "Devil's Domain" as they called it, perhaps they did conjure up La Llorona to the Oasis Ranch?

Chapter Notes

1 Nelson, "The Oasis Ranch," p.1.

2 Ibid, p.42.

3 Koonce, "The Great Oasis Well," *New Mexico Magazine* (August 1966).

4 Kraul & Beatty, *The Weeping Woman*, p.51.

5 Ibid, p.52.

6 Ibid, p.53.

7 Nelson, "The Oasis Ranch," p.43.

8 "The Oasis and its Jewel, the Big Well," p.7. [1950s program given for the Girl Scouts by an unknown author. It was donated to the HSSNM by Clarence Adams in 2000.]

Alejo Herrera, a resdient of Chihuahuita, who lived to be 117 years old.
(HSSNM #3051.)

14.

OLD TIME TALES OF
CHIHUAHUITA

B efore Roswell was put on the map by Van C. Smith, there was a small Spanish village by the name of Rio Hondo in the area. Rio Hondo also predated other proto-Roswell settlements, like Missouri Plaza and Rio Berrendo. It was colonized in the 1850s by Hispanics from Mexico, Northern New Mexico, and Texas. However, unlike its brethren, Rio Hondo never faded away or disappeared. Over the years, it was absorbed into Roswell and eventually became known as Chihuahuita, or "little Chihuahua." The oldest historical district in the confines of Roswell, it comprises about 22 blocks. In 1936, Georgia Redfield described Chihuahua thusly:

> This district incorporated as a part of the city with a population of 1000 Spanish-speaking people, has the colorful atmosphere of a Spanish village. The people living here, in a world all their own, cling to old customs and live in quaint adobe, mud roofed houses, the exteriors made gay in the autumn, with garlands of bright red chili. Chairs in the cleanly swept patios – yards – are usually occupied, afternoons, by the old men and women of the different households, who enjoyed midday siestas in the sun.[1]

Charlie Fowler selling tamales. (HSSNM Larkham Album One, #631)

As the oldest district in town, Chihuahuita was home to many "old-timers" in the 1930s who were interviewed by writers like Redfield about their pasts in the Wild West. One such colorful character who made up the tapestry of Chihuahuita was Charlie Fowler, called "Old Hot Tamale." By his own testimony, Fowler was predominantly Choctaw and was born in 1856. His first job was working for John Chisum in Denton County, Texas. He came with Chisum's first herds into the Roswell region in the late 1860s, though he didn't settle there permanently until the early 1900s. By that time, Fowler was renowned for making tamales, hence his nickname.[2]

Then there was, Alejo Herrera, who resided in Chihuahuita in the later years of his life and lived to be 117 years old, causing some to call him the "Methuselah of Chihuahuita." Herrera, who was born in 1819 and lived until 1936, led an interesting and adventurous life. He was born in Mexico and captured by Apaches at age 11; he did not escape them until age 30 in 1849, when a drunken brawl at the Apache camp finally gave him an opportunity. In his horseback getaway, Herrera also rescued a captive white girl. They both arrived safely in Santa Fe. Later, in the 1870s, Herrera was said to be a brave fighter in the Lincoln County War, and although it wasn't said which side he fought on, he did hide outlaw Billy the Kid from the law twice, once rolled up in his bed roll. In his later years, Herrera took up residence in Chihuahuita and died under the care of friends, Augustin and Lola Garcia, when he passed away from extreme old age.[3]

Then there were community-minded heroes, like Augustin La Riva who, in 1907, began construction on a large wall located around E. Alameda St. in the Chihuahuita district. It was 100 feet long, 13 feet wide, and 18 feet high. For many years, Roswell residents puzzled over the purpose of the wall. It was perfectly straight enclosing nothing so it couldn't serve as an enclosure, and if it marked a boundary of any kind, then what? As usual, it was Redfield who finally dug up the truth on the mysterious wall: La Riva built it to help keep the local youth out of trouble. "We had to make games for the boys in Chihuahua, for they play too much with the cards – what you call it – gambling? They lost money, they never stay home," he told Redfield. And so Riva built the wall for the purpose of playing handball as a distraction other than gambling. He told Redfield:

"Yes, I had the wall made. It was a game – *celota* (handball) – like your boys play with a basket on a wall, only in this game, you do not use a basket, you use only the hands. I pay $400 for making the wall." He continued, "They like the handball game. It gave them much pleasure long time. They tired of it now." La Riva went on to lament the lack of a park in Chihuahuita at the time. "We pay our taxes here long time – 40, 50 years – now we should have a park to keep our boys and girls out of the bad things they find to do, to keep them happy like the wall did once. They tired of playing and we took it down all but the cement part. We can build it up again."

Image of early day Chihuahuita. (HSSNM #3107A)

Another of the more interesting old-timers that Redfield found in Chihuahua was one who told of a lost buried treasure. A source she identified only by the last name of Gorgonio told her, "There is a buried treasure in the Caballo Mountains (Horse Mountains) 35 miles northwest of Las Cruces by a spring under big rocks in Caballo Canyon ..."

He specified that the treasure comprised "gold hunks, and not gold bars" that covered up the spring. He continued, "It was brought there on loaded mules and horses on many, many trips after murdering raids of Apache and Comanche Indians."

Gorgonio told her the complicated circumstances under which he obtained the map. An unnamed man from New Mexico, who had found this treasure, was staying at the home of a woman living in old Mexico. He told her the secret of his buried treasure and also shared with her a map he had made leading to it. However, she became angry with him at one point, stole the map from him, and set off for New Mexico to find it for herself. "She didn't know what to do to find her treasure after she got here. I found her lost, in Carrizozo. I was a good friend to her. She said to me, 'The secret brings to me only bad luck,' (that was because she stole it) so she gave it to me."

Gorgonio intended to use the treasure for the benefit of his family and the Chihuahua community as a whole. "When we find that treasure," said Gorgonio, "we do good for everybody, all the time."[4]

Another photo of early-day Chihuahuita. (HSSNM #3107B)

One story told to this author while collecting tales for *The New Mexico Book of Witches* turned up a suspected *bruja* in the neighborhood. Years ago, probably around the 1950s, an old woman suspected of being a witch broke into one of the churches. Her objective was to steal candle wax, as it was said that voodoo dolls could be made with wax from the church. She was successful in stealing the wax, however, she was attacked and killed by neighborhood dogs on her way home. Chihuahuita was notorious for unleashed dogs running around the neighborhoods, the teller of the story explained, but not very many attacked without provocation. Therefore, the teller of the tale implied, the usually peaceable dogs were acting in the neighborhood's best interests when they did away with the old witch. Ultimately, these are only a handful of the folkloric tales from Chihuahuita.

Chapter Notes

[1] Redfield, "Roswell Chihuahua District," December 8, 1936.
[2] Fleming & Williams, *Treasures of History II*, pp.161-163.
[3] Fleming & Williams, *Treasures of History III*, pp.20-23.
[4] Redfield, "Buried treasure folktales in Chihuahua district of Roswell," *Roswell Morning Dispatch* (March 1940), p.6.

15.

THE DAY ROSWELL WAS
DOOMED

Back in the 1980s, another beloved Roswell historian, Clarence Adams, published a newsletter entitled *The Old Timers Review*. In it were tales sprawling all of Southeastern New Mexico, but more often than not pertained to Chaves County. Many jewels in the footnotes of Chaves County's history were printed, among them a story about how back in the mid-1930s, during the Great Depression, a woman claiming to be a prophet predicted that Roswell was doomed. She said the town would be swallowed up into the ground, sending some spooked residents to higher ground on Six-Mile Hill for the night. The event occurred in the summer of 1936 and Adams remembered that,

> Earlier that week we had heard that some lady, who claimed to be a prophet, had made a prediction that Roswell was "doomed to destruction" and this was to be the night it would happen. She hadn't given the exact details, but I believe she said an earthquake would cause the ground to "open up and swallow" our town.[1]

Adams joked, "It really hadn't scared me very much. I'd always been taught that whenever the Lord wanted to bring destruction on a town, He'd do it without any help from some crackpot."

Adams recalled how his father came home and mentioned that he knew of several people who "had made plans to camp on Six-Mile Hill that night." When Clarence's brother, J.B., came home, he gave a more dramatic update. He said that he had seen many people leaving Roswell and that "the highway out of town going west is packed with cars – and they say that the bathhouse at Bottomless Lakes is already a foot underwater!"

Roswell about the year 1930. (HSSNM #508)

Clarence's father dismissed the hype but he did note that as it grew darker that evening they could see the lights of many cars by the dozens moving west in a long string going for Six-Mile Hill. "Crazy people!" Clarence's father exclaimed. "Wonder what this world coming to?"

Adams went to bed with only a bit of anxiety that night. As he looked up at the stars he mused that if it was God's will to swallow up Roswell, then so be it.

Adams concluded,

I often think about that night that so many people left Roswell for a "safer" place. However, the strangest thing happened after that. You couldn't find a single soul in the whole community who'd left town on that fateful night. Often you'd hear a conversation which went like this:

"You take off for the hills the other night when Roswell was supposed to sink?"

"Naw, shore didn't. Stayed right at home. Don't believe in that kind of nonsense."

"Well, I reckon a lot of folks took off for high country anyway," would come the answer.

"Not me – them people was crazy. Anybody with any sense at all wouldn't pay no mind to some old crack-pot woman like that."

Clarence Adams. (Courtesy HSSNM)

However, the idea of Roswell being destroyed wasn't a foreign one to early day residents like Clarence Adams. In 1991, after a tremor shook Roswell, Adams took to the papers to reminisce about an earthquake that occurred in Roswell in the year 1931. He remembered how he awoke that morning with his bed rattling and was terrified at the time that his house might've been haunted. "Boy, was I relieved when our neighbor informed us that we had really experienced an earthquake! Why, dishes rattled and walls shook at their house, he said. Afterwards we heard all sorts of stories having to do with that strange experience." To corroborate the story, Adams consulted with fellow old-timers Ernestine Chester Williams and Ivan Gill, who also remembered an earthquake in the very early 1930s.

So, with the memory of the 1931 earthquake still fresh for many Roswellites in 1936, it's understandable that some took the doomsday woman's predictions to heart.

Chapter Notes

---

[1] Adams, "Where were you the day Roswell was 'doomed?,'" *Old Timers Review* (Vol.4 No.4).

16.
LEGEND OF DIAMOND CAVE

N ew Mexico has been a land of lost treasures ever since the Spanish conquistadors set foot here in search of the Seven Cities of Gold. If there's one unique treasure spot within the confines of Chaves County, it's a mysterious locale known only as "Diamond Cave." In the archives of the Historical Society for Southeastern New Mexico exists a handwritten document by Maurice G. Fulton detailing "Diamond Cave" dated November 29, 1936:

> This cave is the subject of various treasures and romance. One such story has it that in the early days some real diamonds were found in the mouth of the cave. Another story is that a Mexican was murdered for wages which had been paid to him and the money hidden in the cave. Still another says an Indian hid valuables and other things in this cave. And some say there are red (blood) hand prints on some of the rocks in the cave. After all this story-telling I have heard of several people going into the cave but have not been able to find them to talk to them. Without the stories and legends it is an interesting place. It is a gypsum sink which abounds in the county around for a long ways. It is roughly circular about 200 yards across and about 150 feet deep, tapering toward the bottom to a hole just large enough to crawl into.

The original document.

Another article claimed that Diamond Cave was located "somewhere in the barren terrain of the Half Way House country, in a split distance between Roswell and Torrance." The article went on to tell of a group of cowhands out on the trail. The cook found a piece of "pretty glass" which he later took to San Antonio, Texas, where it was appraised as a "true diamond." Another newspaper clippings from Roswell in the mid-1930s further enlightened on the cave:

For years we have heard rumors of a diamond cave about forty or fifty miles north of Roswell. The stories have it that some diamonds were actually found in the cave and were taken to Dallas and sold to jewelers there and were pronounced real diamonds. As to the truth of the stories we cannot say, but we did get some firsthand information from Mr. Earickson on the cave, for at one time years ago he had actually been in it.

He was one of a small party entering the cave. One of the party was a government mineral expert. They made their way inside through a small entrance barely large enough to admit a large man but found large cavities within. They were gone for hours and believed they had gone down probably two thousand feet. It required an hour and a half to make the return trip. They had to use ropes in many places to ascend or descend. The air near the bottom was found to be quite bad and often extinguished the lights of their lanterns.

The mineral expert said he saw no indications of diamonds but declared there was an immense amount of pure plaster of paris within the cave. Some chambers were found that were large enough to hold a large building.

Another story about this cave that seems to be rumor is that one man found the diamonds there and actually had them pronounced to be diamonds and sold them as such.

Anyway, it is evident that there is a big cave up north of Roswell, whether it is of value or not.[1]

The article's opening sentence clarified that the cave was "forty or fifty miles north of Roswell…" If this is true, then it lines up perfectly with the little settlement of Mesa, one of the more mysterious spots that one encounters in the laborious stretch between Roswell and Vaughn. In the words of Guy Crandall and George Parsons in the *Old-Timers Review*, "[Mesa] appears to be perched on top of the world, a tiny oasis surrounded by miles of rolling rangeland."[2]

George Parsons and his wife for many years managed the lone convenience store that defined Mesa. The little place began in 1932 when Parsons was fleeing the dustbowl of Oklahoma. Parsons told Crandall that he knew of "some fellers back in the 30s who drilled for diamonds not far from here…"

Crandall shook his head in disbelief, and Parsons replied, "I know it for a fact, because I sold the fellers gas for a drilling rig!"

Parson made up some fun folklore as to the birth of the mesa. He claimed that because he and his neighbors had no privacy, that "each one of us got a wheelbarrow and piled up dirt until we built that Mesa." (HSSNM #2820)

Parsons continued on about another treasure-hunting excursion in the region. Parsons said that in the late 1930s, Roswell resident Fred Miles would often stop at his store with his wife and a Hispanic sheep rancher. Parsons knew the trio was up to something interesting because they would often appear at the store early in the morning heading north and reappear later that afternoon on their way back south to Roswell. Eventually, Parsons asked him what they were up to, and Miles showed him a sack of golden nuggets. Miles explained that one of the ranchman's herders had found gold about seven miles northwest of Mesa a year prior.

Maj. M.G Fulton

The Long Canyon into Diamond Cave

11
29
36

On November 29, 1936, Maurice Fulton found Diamond Cave for himself, but apparently no diamonds or gold. (HSSNM #1485B)

The herder had unloaded a railroad car of sheep at Yeso, which is today regarded as nothing more than a ghost town near Fort Sumner. He herded the sheep south from Yeso through a dense fog. Due to the low visibility, he tripped and fell when his foot caught in what he thought was a prairie dog hole. When he looked down at the hole, something that glittered caught his eye. Hoping it was gold, he gathered the glittering substance and put it in a sack. Wanting to return, he looked around for notable landmarks to help him remember the exact area. However, due to the dense fog, he couldn't discern any, plus his sheep were wandering off and he needed to catch up with them. The herder later mentioned his find to the rancher to which the land belonged. The rancher, in turn, eventually connected with Miles, who authenticated the gold for him. After that, they joined forces to try to find the treasure.

Of the situation, Crandall surmised,

> I believe the story George Parsons told about the gold, and I think the people involved were on the level. But how did the gold get in the prairie dog hole? The country around Mesa doesn't appear to be mineralized. It could be that the Mexican miscalculated the location of his find – which was very possible. Perhaps there is some other logical explanation of how the gold got there. I don't know.[3]

It's interesting that Crandall was unaware of the story of Diamond Cave and, therefore, was unable to connect the two, but they would seem to be connected nonetheless. Perhaps Diamond Cave still lies somewhere near Mesa, just waiting to be found...

Chapter Notes

[1] Clipped article dated March 19, 1936. [HSSNM Archives]
[2] Crandal, "We Built a Mesa," *Old Timer's Review* (Vol.1, No.4).
[3] Ibid.

HAUNTED TREASURE HOLE OUTSIDE OF ROSWELL

This tale, collected by Manuel Berg in the 1930s and given to him by a man identified only as Pacheco out of Albuquerque, may have related to the treasure of Diamond Cave and the other strange spots around Mesa. Instead of paraphrasing, here is the tale in Pacheco's own words of a haunted treasure hole somewhere near Roswell:

"What I am about to tell you happened in the country around Roswell. There were three men, sheepherders, and one of the three was the foreman. They were in charge of a large flock of sheep and they very seldom came to town. At least they didn't ever get to town more than four or five times a year. This which I am telling was told by the foreman, and they all swore that it was the truth. Here is what the foreman said: "It was very late one night when I started to look for my two men, Pablo and Carlos. The stars weren't out and a strong wind had come up and I wanted to know whether the sheep were in a good shelter. You see, if they are not sheltered they become kind of wild and we have a lot of trouble gathering them together again. It took me a long time to find the two men because they had also read the signs that a storm was coming up and had herded all the sheep into a little valley.

"When I did find the men they were trying to make a small fire but were having a little trouble. I helped them start the fire and put some coffee to heat. It was very cold and we weren't through with our coffee when it began to rain and blow real bad. We very quickly stamped the fire out and ran to find some better shelter for ourselves. We had already taken care of the sheep so we didn't bother about them. The three of us must have become separated because I soon heard an awful scream nearby and stopped to try and locate it. I called for Pablo and Carlos but only Pablo answered me and then came running over to see me. Carlos had gotten lost. We couldn't leave Carlos alone because one never knows what can happen to a person alone in the desert so we went back to where the fire had been and began to search. We searched very close to the ground, almost crawling on our hands and knees and even that way I almost fell into this hole. I was very scared when I found the hole but I called out if Carlos was there and he answered my call. Pablo came up to me and then we called to him again to find if there was anything we could do to help him. He, Carlos, said for us to tie a candle and some matches to a cord and lower it and at the same time to light a match so he could see where the entrance was. We did this and pretty soon we felt a jerk of the rope and knew he had found the candle.

"Pretty soon a dim light came from this hole in the ground but we couldn't see anything from the top—I mean we couldn't make out anything that was down there. I called to Carlos that we would throw the end of a lariat down and then pull him up if he couldn't come up any other way. He said to wait a little bit because he had seen something which he wanted to investigate closer. Next thing he calls up to us and says that he has found a great number of sacks and boxes filled with money both gold and silver. While we were talking, Carlos at the bottom of this hole and Pablo and I at the top, Carlos' light went out and we heard a strange voice say 'Don't be afraid. Many men have died for this treasure and many more are going to die'—and the voice began to laugh, a laugh so horrible that we almost fainted; that is, Pablo and I. Maybe Carlos did faint. Very much shaken I called to Carlos if he had the end of the lariat so we could pull him up. We didn't get an answer right away. Then we saw a light again and Carlos' voice said that he was coming up right away but first he would try to bring one of the sacks of money up with him. This time Carlos tied the lariat around his body and walked further into the cave. Then Carlos said that even one sack was so heavy that he couldn't lift it up. As he said this the candle went out again and the strange voice began to laugh, a laugh that makes my blood run cold and many times I wake up in the night and my heart is filled with great fear. After several moments the laughter died down and the voice said in a deep rumbling tone, 'You will never be able to take one sack. You must take the whole treasure at once or else nothing.'

"I know that Carlos fainted this time because we felt a strong pull at the lariat and frightened as we were we began to pull it up. It was a very hard job to pull Carlos up because he weighed almost two hundred pounds, and first we had to drag his body across the floor of the cave. By the time we got Carlos out, he had come to life again but he was a very sick man. He had a high fever and we got our horses and tied him onto his and came into town. Carlos never did get over his sickness. Within two weeks he was dead. Now Carlos being gone did not upset me a great deal because I thought it might have been a natural death but when Pablo became sick right after Carlos was buried, I became worried. I quit my job and left that part of the country but later I heard that Pablo had also died and his last words were that he had been cursed by an evil voice."

"Now," Mr. Pacheco said, "that is a story I heard from this man who lives in Martines town in Albuquerque. This man also says that he has a map showing just where this treasure is hidden but I have never seen this map. When I asked him why he didn't go again to get the treasure, he said that since Pablo and Carlos were dead and he still lived, he preferred to go on living and let somebody else find the cursed treasure."

17.
LILY KLASNER
THE LADY OUTLAW

Buried in Roswell's South Park Cemetery is someone who could be considered an unsung hero of the Wild West. As her obituary put it, Lily Casey Klasner, who died in Roswell on June 3, 1946, "lived side by side with outlaws and Indians and could hold her own with any of them." Lily was born in Mason County, Texas, in 1862, and came of age during the Lincoln County War. Her contemporaries spoke highly of her. For instance, Nib Jones remembered, "She stayed with us. She always wore an apron; and in that apron she always carried a 45. And boy, could she get it out!"[1] The great "frontier fighter" George Coe said, "Calamity Jane didn't have anything on Lily Klasner."

Lily was tough as nails, and rather than swooning over Billy the Kid, she was head-over-heels for his jailer, Pecos Bob Olinger. Lily was likely regarded as "un-lady-like" by many, and she also tried for murder at one time. Eve Ball probably summed Lily up more objectively to Leon Metz. She explained to him that "when Lily was thirteen, her father was killed... So she grew up fighting and working like a man, capable and shrewd."[2] Ball further explained, "Mrs. Casey [the mother] was an invalid, a cripple, and Lily's two older brothers she described as puny, Will and Ad. ... When she was about thirteen, she became the defender of the family. And boy, she was thorough and efficient at it, too."[3]

Above is pictured Lily on her wedding day to Joe Klasner.

Roswellite Cecil Bonney also remembered semi-fondly how Lily would literally "ride shotgun" while on the road between Roswell and nearby Picacho. In those days, it was a narrow road that gave nary enough room for two buggies at the same time. As a courtesy, one driver would usually pull over so that the other could pass safely. Not Lily. She kept the high ground at all times. Bonney remembered once in the 1890s that, "Regardless of the direction she was traveling, Lily kept to the upper—the safe—side of the road. Her right of way was established by the single-barrel, 12-gauge shotgun she held across her lap with one hand while she drove with the other."[4]

The old Picacho highway. (HSSNM #2693B)

To digress, and as most Lincoln County War enthusiasts know, Lily's family moved to the Ruidoso region of New Mexico before the onslaught of the Lincoln County War. Though it was the death of John Tunstall that truly kicked off the war, many would argue that the murder of Lily's father was an important precursor to it as well. As Eve Ball related to Leon Metz earlier, after her father's death, Lily found herself taking a leadership role in her family. That's another reason that Lily's 1946 obituary said she was "truly a woman of the West" living in an era when there "was no law and order and most of the travelers were outlaws..."[5]

As stated earlier, unlike many of her contemporaries, Lily had no love for Billy the Kid, possibly due to her close association with the Chisum family, who other than Sallie didn't have fond memories of the outlaw. On that note, some even said Lily had a childhood crush on John Chisum and would like to have married him when she grew up. Instead, Lily married Joe Klasner, a bridge builder and repairman for J.J. Hagerman. Lily met Joe, said to be a large man, while she was working as a telegrapher along the Mexican border and they were later wed in Laredo.

The Klasner homestead in the Hondo Valley.

It was sometime after the marriage in the year 1896 that Lily, Joe, and her brother, Robert "Ad" Casey, found themselves embroiled in a water dispute. And, in the "Land of Little Rain," water was serious business. The matter went to court in the office of the Justice of the Peace at Picacho. A U.S. Marshall named Buck Guyse was doing his best on the witness stand to defend a ranch hand, George White, accused of illegally appropriating water from Robert Casey.

According to the *Roswell Daily Record*, the Caseys had a one third interest in a ditch that White used water from and thus had him arrested.[6] White, it should be noted, was not in the courtroom, and so he was spared the violence to follow. As it was, the constable was out at the moment, leaving Guyse and one unnamed witness alone in the courtroom with Ad, Joe, Lily, and their impressionable eighteen-year-old hired hand, James Brown. Brown was reading a statement relating to the charges when Ad Casey called Guyse a "damned liar." Guyse jumped up to confront Ad, and the latter grabbed Guyse's gun.

Then, what the papers initially reported as several men grabbed Guyse and held him by the arms while Ad shot him. After Guyse had fallen to the floor from the first gunshot, Ad shot him twice more to ensure that he was dead.

Ad Casey at the old Casey homestead. (HSSNM #1444E)

However, soon rumors began to spread that Lily had a hand in the killing. Cecil Bonney remembered, "The story I heard at the time was that [Lily] held Guyse while her brother Ad did the shooting. Later it was said that Ad, who was partially paralyzed, did the holding and Lily did the shooting."[7]

The rumors had some truth to them and the press sensationalized Lily's part in the killing via the headline: "HELD BY A WOMAN A Female Involved in the Murder of Deputy United States Marshal Buck Guyse at Picacho". The report indicated that not only did Lily help hold down Guyse, she also overpowered and pushed the unnamed witness out the door of the courtroom. In the papers, Lily would later claim that she did so because the man, a staunch supporter of Guyse, attempted to draw a weapon.[8]

Actually, many old-time ranchers didn't blame Lily at all. Nib Jones stated, "When they had a trial in those days it was not to determine whether or not the men was guilty of shooting the other – it was to decide if he was justified; and if so, the verdict was not guilty."

Nib continued,

> Lil killed Buck Guise on the witness stand. This trial was over her claim, the Circle Diamond. Diamond A were trying to get Lil out and Buck Guyse was trying to get her out. Another case of persecution instead of prosecution. Didn't do anything to her – he had it coming to him. You stick your neck out and you will get it cut off.[9]

This story was hotly contested in a hearing at the courthouse in Lincoln at a later date. "This case has attracted a great deal of attention, and the interest has been so intense as to virtually divide the people of the neighborhood into two bitter factions, composed of the friends and the enemies of the accused," the *Albuquerque Journal* of May 11, 1896 reported.[10] The trial in Lincoln was overseen by Judge Laughlin, and none other than A.B. Fall presided over the prosecution. In the end, Ad Casey was sentenced to 15 years in the penitentiary while the Klasners were acquitted.

Perhaps this incident was partly to blame for the Klasner's getting divorced some time afterwards. After she was shed of her husband, Lily began visiting nearby Roswell to see old friend Sallie Chisum. The two were endeavoring to co-author a book on the Lincoln County War together, and in 1904 the two took a research trip to Santa Fe. However, Sallie eventually lost interest in the project according to Eve Ball, and Lily took it over. In addition to writing about Billy the Kid and the war, Lily, despite now being in her late forties, took up some of the Kid's former depredations, namely cattle rustling. The *Roswell Daily Record* of September 4, 1909, reported:

> Mrs. Klasner Under Arrest.
> Word has come of the arrest of Mrs. L.C. Klasner in Lincoln county on the charge of conspiring with two Mexicans to steal some calves [sic] belanging to various ranching outfits west of here. Mrs. Klasner is well known in Roswell and has many friends here who hope that the charge will prove to be without foundation in fact.

Sophie Poe, another Roswell old-timer, had what we would today call a "hot take" on Lily as well. Sophie, it should be noted, was a friend of Buck Guyse, the deceased, who according to her had some cattle stolen by the Casey family. Per Sophie Poe, who clearly was misremembering the events somewhat, "When he went to get them, [the cattle] he was killed. It is believed Lily Casey shot him, although her brother took the blame and was sent to prison."[11]

In 1912, it appears yet another cattle rustling incident occurred which was taken to court in 1914. *The Albuquerque Journal* of October 13, 1914, reported in the story "Mrs. Lily Klasner Cited for Contempt" that she had positioned herself near the door of the quarters of the grand jury to listen in on their deliberations! She was caught by one of the jurors who stepped outside suddenly and unexpectedly and was cited for contempt as the article suggested. Lily was actually in court for two separate matters at once. In the case of the State vs. Lily Klasner over the cattle larceny charges, Lily was found guilty. In the case of Miller vs. Klasner, another water dispute, Klasner was found not guilty, however. Klasner's story picked up again in the papers that December, in the *Albuquerque Morning Journal* of December 2, 1914, which called her a

Lincoln County Pioneer. It explained that "the defendant found herself in the embarrassing position that the calves in question were found enclosed in a small alfalfa pasture"[12] on her property.

In the end, Governor McDonald pardoned Lily for the 1912 accusations of cattle rustling which she was set to serve three to four years for in the state penitentiary. McDonald stated in his pardon that Lily was "in such a state of health that any such imprisonment would probably be disastrous to her, both physically and mentally."[13]

McDonald issued this pardon on the condition that Lily leave the state of New Mexico and never return. This Lily, to her credit, did not do. She was a staple of the territory, and here she remained—the governor's orders be damned. Or so went one story. According to Sophie Poe, the widow of John W. Poe (Garrett's deputy the night he shot the Kid): "Governor McDonald told Lily to stay out of New Mexico for the next ten years. She went to a convent at El Paso and received some education. As the governor lay dying, she forced her way into his room and cursed him."[14]

At some point, Lily finally finished the book she had started with Sallie Chisum, which was really just Lily's perspective on the Lincoln County War. As it turned out, it wouldn't see publication until after her death as *My Girlhood Among Outlaws* with the help of Eve Ball, the beloved chronicler of the Ruidoso region. However, before Ball, Lily had actually passed the book along to Maurice G. Fulton. A respected historian known for accuracy, Fulton had by this time produced an annotated edition of Pat Garrett's mostly inauthentic *The Authentic Life of Billy the Kid*, pointing out and correcting many of its fallacies in his annotations. Later, Sophie Poe asked Fulton to edit her husband's manuscript, *The Death of Billy the Kid*. This Fulton did and landed him on the radar of Lily, who had finished her memoirs some time ago but was aware that they were not publication ready. (Some have described her first draft as being only semi-literate.)

In the hope of learning heretofore unknown accounts of the Lincoln County War, Fulton readily agreed to edit the manuscript. But whereas Lily only wanted Fulton to edit it for grammar and structure, as he had done Poe's *Death of Billy the Kid*, Fulton wanted to point out the differences between Klasner's recollection of events and her own opinions from historical fact. In researching public records on the Casey family in Carrizozo (by then the county seat of Lincoln) and Santa Fe, Fulton learned some unflattering details about the Caseys. Ever the accurate scholar, Fulton apparently included some of these details in his version of the manuscript, which Lily eventually saw. Authors William E. Gibbs and Alfred L. Castle summed it up the best in their article on Fulton's career in a 1980 issue of *New Mexico Historical Review.*

> The cantankerous Lil, after reading a carbon copy of Fulton's editorial work, did not appreciate his efforts. Unlike William Bonney [Billy the Kid], she was alive and unwilling to accept the professor's reconstruction of her and her family's roles in the history of the region.[15]

Maurice G. Fulton.

One summer evening, Fulton was working in his basement office at Wilson Hall at New Mexico Military Institute in Roswell when he received a surprise visit from Lily. Hearing someone coming down the hall, he looked up to see Lily pointing a forty-five at him. Her demands were simple, hand back the copy of her manuscript that he had edited so that he couldn't publish it. Fulton clearly believed that Lily was capable of pulling the trigger, and so handed off the manuscript to her and she went on her way.

After the incident with Fulton, Lily tried again at handing the manuscript over, this time to Eric Bruce, then the principal at the Lincoln school. This didn't pan out either, and after Lily passed in 1946, the manuscript was crammed under Lily's wedding dress in an old trunk. Finding the trunk was something of a treasure hunt for historians, with Ball being told about the manuscript by Fulton. Via descendants of the Coes and Caseys, the trunk was located in an old, abandoned adobe house in the Hondo Valley and the manuscript given to Ball.

Ball, being diplomatic in her introduction to the book, wrote that "Colonel Fulton was unable to complete this contract for publication so this contract was dissolved in 1929…"[16] (And yes, Ball did know the truth, as Fulton told her himself about what had happened.) What scandalous revelations Fulton included in his version of the book we do not know for sure. According to Sophie Poe, Fulton said that Klasner's manuscript "[did] not mince words and [would] cause a lot of friction if printed."[17]

Of course, today, to a lesser degree, that would no longer be true. But back in Fulton's time, talk of who killed who and who was justified in the Lincoln County War could have led to further violence. Anyhow, if you ever find yourself strolling through South Park Cemetery, stop and pay your respects to an oft neglected female outlaw, Roswell's own Calamity Jane, Lily Casey Klasner.

Chapter Notes

---

[1] Nib Jones to Eve Ball. [MSS 3096 Box 14 Folder 2]

[2] Leon Metz Interview with Eve Ball (5-14-1969), p.10.

[3] Ibid, pp.8-9.

[4] Bonney, *Looking Over My Shoulder*, p.158.

[5] Ball, *My Girlhood Among Outlaws*, p.4.

[6] "Killed With His Own Gun," *Albuquerque Journal*, May 5, 1896. This article cited information from the *Roswell Daily Record* (no date given).

[7] Bonney, *Looking Over My Shoulder*, p.159.

[8] In his article, "Who Killed Who in Lincoln County, N.M.," published in the *Lincoln County News* of July 17, 1969, respected historian Philip J. Rasch did recount the murder of Guyse and Lily Klasner's association with it. In his section on Guyse, Rasch wrote that several informants had told him that Lily actually slit Guyse's throat in the courtroom and that her brother took the blame for her! Rasch made it clear that contemporary accounts gave no indication of any such thing though, and that coroner's reports clearly showed that Guyse died of gunshot wounds.

[9] Nib Jones to Eve Ball. [MSS 3096 Box 14 Folder 2]

[10] "CASEY MURDER TRIAL," *Albuquerque Journal*, May 11, 1896.

[11] Ibid.

[12] "MRS. KLASNER LOSES OUT IN FINAL HEARING," *Albuquerque Morning Journal*, December 2, 1914.

[13] "LINCOLN COUNTY WOMAN PARDONED," *Carrizozo Outlook*, March 12, 1915.

[14] "Notes on an interview with Mrs. Sophie," April 19, 1947. [From the Robert N. Mullin Collection]

[15] Gibbs and Castle, "Maurice Garland Fulton," *New Mexico Historical Review* (Vol. 55, No.2 1980), p.125.

[16] Ball, *My Girlhood Among Outlaws*, p.2.

[17] "Notes on an interview with Mrs. Sophie," April 19, 1947. [From the Robert N. Mullin Collection]

ALLIGATOR OF THE BERRENDO

As strange as this may sound, Chaves County used to have a few alligators crawling around. While these may seem like tall tales, not only are the sources of the stories reliable, there is even photographic proof of the "Alligator of the Berrendo."

The late historian Elvis E. Fleming related to this author a tale told to him by his sister concerning her youth in Roswell. Fleming's sister claimed that on the grounds at NMMI she was with a friend one night when she stopped and rested her foot upon a rock. According to her, the "rock" opened its eyes and was actually an alligator!

Before that, an alligator was often seen roaming the Berrendo River. Lowry Hagerman, a longtime resident of the Pecos Valley and descendant of J. J. Hagerman, spoke of the alligator in an interview taken in the mid-1980s:

> Hagerman: I saw a six foot alligator in the Berrendo [River].
> Interviewer: Who put the alligator in the Berrendo River? Somebody had to have…
> Hagerman: Oh, I don't know. The alligator came up the Pecos, you know, in the summer time. Maybe someone had a pet and turned it loose. I never knew. Never could find out. Never took much interest in it really. But the alligator was there.

Though that was unverified for years, the Historical Society for Southeast New Mexico was eventually given a photo of the creature as proof, which can be seen on this page.

19.
MIRACLES OF SAINT MARY'S

Sometime in 1906, construction began on Saint Mary's Hospital, Roswell's first. The hospital was built by the Sisters of the Sorrowful Mother, headed by Reverend Mother Boniface, for a cost of $20,000. Mother Boniface had come to Roswell in 1906 from Wisconsin to look into starting a hospital and sanitarium for the town. For close to a century thereafter, Saint Mary's was a beloved fixture of Roswell until it was torn down. During its lifetime, the hospital was privy to some miraculous happenings.

For instance, during the fateful summer of 1947 that would eventually catapult Roswell to fame worldwide, two nuns at Saint Mary's, Mother Superior Mary Bernadette and Sister Capistrano, watched a fiery object descend towards the horizon north of town. It occurred late in the hours of July 4th around the same time that a flying saucer allegedly crashed north of town. Did the sisters see the famous saucer as it was crashing, or was it merely an unrelated UFO sighting?[1]

A few years prior to the 1947 UFO sighting, Saint Mary's was home to what may have been a bonafide miracle. "It happened many years ago, and at that time we were told that to be an authentic miracle, the doctor on the case had to testify that it was a miracle," remembered Sister M. Agnella Caduff many years later. "Well, the doctor on the case was an atheist and did not believe in miracles, but in my mind it was a true miracle."[2]

It was the year 1944, and the patient was a man who suffered badly from Buerger's disease which caused unbearable pain.[3] The disease also necessitated that the poor man have his foot amputated one night, just below the ankle. Even worse, gangrene had spread, necessitating the amputation of his leg just above the knee the next morning at 8AM. The poor man was in agony from his disease, but already had so many narcotics in his system that he couldn't be allowed to have any more. That's where Sister Caduff came in. At 11:30 PM that night, she heard the patient crying in distress. Knowing he couldn't be administered any more pain killers, she asked the man permission to pin a medal of Mother Francis on the bandage where the stump of his foot was. Although he wasn't Catholic, he agreed, and Sister Caduff went with the man's wife to the chapel to pray for him at midnight. There they asked "the Good Lord through the intercession of Mother Francis for a miracle."

Saint Mary's c.1906. (HSSNM #188A)

To everyone's shock, the next morning, the patient was found in a pain-free state. Not only that, the wound that necessitated that his leg be amputated had been completely healed. Just to be safe, the man was kept there for four more days. After the four days, he was released, his leg still attached. The operation had been canceled. Sister Caduff, the patient, and his wife all agreed it was a true miracle. However, Sister Caduff couldn't get the two doctors who had done the foot amputation, and who were scheduled to amputate the leg, to agree.

THE GROTTO AT SAINT MARY'S

Saint Mary's also used to house a beautiful grotto which was modeled after the site of another miracle; that of The Immaculate Conception. Back in Lourdes, France, on February 11, 1858, a fourteen-year-old shepherd girl was tending to her flock in the Pyrenees Mountains when she saw an apparition of the Virgin Mary. The girl's name was Bernadette Soubirous and she claimed to see a woman in white with a blue sash in a cave high up on the mountainside. The figure said to her, "I am The Immaculate Conception," and instructed her to dig for a spring in an unlikely spot. When the girl dug into the sand, water began to flow, and later people who washed in the spring told of miraculous healings. A chapel was also built on the spot, and many considered it to be the second most holy spot in all Catholicism after the Vatican itself. In Roswell, with no nearby caves to pray in, the Sisters brought in rocks to construct their own cave grotto. Outside they planted pecan trees and shrubs, and most importantly, installed a replica of the famous statue "Our Lady of Lourdes" in a niche above the grotto.

In a report, Sister Caduff recollected Dr. Joe Williams, a Southern Baptist, and Dr. Fall, a 33rd Degree Mason, "would not admit that there was anything miraculous about the man's sudden recovery, though they could give no explanation of it." The Southern Baptist was a bit more open, stating that after five years had passed he would consider signing something to that effect, if the patient's disease never flared up again. However, five years later, he reneged and didn't want to sign anything. Sister Caduff recollected that she saw the patient around town for the next nine years until she left in 1953. She said that the man had never had trouble with his leg again.

In recent years, efforts have resumed to get the Vatican to declare the incident an official miracle in the eyes of the Church.

Chapter Notes

---

[1] It should be noted that the Sisters' sighting did not occur on the night of the famous Wilmot family sighting, which would have been July 2. Most ufologists consider July 2nd to have been the night of the fateful crash, not July 4th, hence why the sighting from Saint Mary's was possibly a separate incident.

[2] Statement written in April 1959 as "Mother Francis Helps".

[3] Patient's name withheld for privacy.

20.
GHOSTS OF
WAFB

For many years, Roswell and Chaves County was defined by its military presence in the form of Walker Air Force Base. The army began negotiations with the Roswell Chamber of Commerce to build an air base in June of 1941, where the army toured a vacant stretch of land south of town as a possible location. By September 1, 1941, construction began for what would first be called the Roswell Army Flying School, and after the bombing of Pearl Harbor on December 7, 1941, construction at the base was sped up so as to make it operational as soon as possible.

The Roswell Air Field was completed and operational by May of 1942, but the name was altered to become the Roswell Army Air Field after a bombardier school was added. For bombardier training at the base, practice bombs with only three pounds of black powder were dropped so that the pilots could see a spark of light, determine how accurate their drop was, and keep noise down to a minimum so as not to bother nearby Roswellites. The practice bombs were dropped on small sheds as well as makeshift boats and buildings. Later, a separate bombing range consisting of 960 acres was commissioned where high explosive demolition bombs could be dropped.

Though it was only initially meant to replace Moffett Field in California, which was being transferred to the Navy, the Roswell Army Air Field went on to become one of the most prestigious bases of its kind after the end of World War II. This is because the RAAF became home to the 509th Bomb Group, the only atomic bomb unit in the world at the time. Roswell accepted the base very enthusiastically and even threw a parade in its honor when it first came to town. The base, eventually renamed Walker Air Force Base, would end up being a valuable asset in Roswell's growth and economy. From the early 1940s into the 1960s, Roswell's population tripled.

Around the same time that the base was built, a Prisoner of War Camp was constructed between Roswell and Dexter and called Orchard Park P.O.W. Camp by locals, even though its official name was the Roswell Prisoner of War Internment Camp. The first German prisoners arrived on November 26, 1942, and another four thousand would follow by August of 1943. The POW camp at Orchard Park was one of the largest detention centers of its kind in the United States during World War II and encompassed 120 acres. The camp was surrounded by barbed wire fences and nearly a dozen guard towers. Escape attempts were rare, although the guards did once find a tunnel dug by the prisoners and filled it back in. The camp housed 4,800 prisoners, with three main compounds housing 1,600 POWs each. The camp also had four doctors, two dentists, seven nurses, and an optician in a 250-bed hospital.

POWs lining the Hondo River in Roswell with rock. (HSSNM #1093C)

From both the base and the POW camp stemmed some ghost stories, one of which was truly out of this world, but we'll start with the POWs. Long after Orchard Park was decommissioned as a POW camp, a boy scout troupe chose to camp there one night. Sitting around the campfire, the scout leader, who had been stationed at WAFB during WWII, told the boys a tale of a young, homesick German POW. Of all the prisoners at the camp, he was the one most determined to escape. Once, it was said, he tunneled out of the barracks and made it all the way to Artesia before he was caught. He made another escape attempt while he was out on a work detail. After that, he was placed in solitary confinement for a time. The young man made a third escape attempt by scaling the barbed wire fence. In doing so, he suffered severe lacerations trying to scale the fence and was taken down and apprehended once more. A final warning was issued that his next attempt would be his last. Next time, he would be shot.

On a fateful, blustery day with low visibility, he decided the dirt storm might conceal him as he scaled the fence again. It didn't. The guards spotted him and shot him as he clung to the fence, and the young POW was no more. For the next two decades, during which the old barracks still stood, visitors swore that on dirty, windy days, they could see his shadow walking through the wind. In the words of *Vision Magazine*: "...when the spring winds begin to howl across southeast New Mexico, and the dust becomes thick in the air, you might want to stay far away from the old Orchard Park POW camp..."[1]

View of Orchard Park POW Camp.

The airbase had its share of ghost stories as well. Like the ghost of the German POW, the ghosts of WAFB were created on a low visibility day as well. In that case, three young airmen were taking off on the runway on a misty morning when visibility was poor. Tragically, their plane crashed and they burned to death. Thereafter, their ghosts were sometimes seen on the southwest end of the runway. As such, superstitious pilots considered it a bad omen if the figures were seen on a cloudy morning. If so, then takeoffs would not be attempted. However, if on those same cloudy mornings no specters were seen, it was considered safe to take off.

However, there was no place that could match the colorful cast of ghostly characters that inhabited the New Mexico Rehabilitation Center (NMRC), which was built on the site of the old base hospital. There was "Old Scratch," a TB patient who could be heard scratching on the door of Room 002. There was a bombardier who appeared from time to time in Room 209 to offer words of encouragement to the patients. There was also a cigarette-smoking man who lit up occasionally in Room 204, a blonde nurse who liked to boss folks around, plus the sounds of crying babies coming from where the old maternity ward used to be.

Aerial view of WAFB. (HSSNM #4610B)

David Rocha, who worked at the NMRC for more than 25 years, remembered one Christmas when all of the other employees had been sent home and only he and a handful of others stayed behind for maintenance and security. All through the night, elevators mysteriously opened and closed, doors would occasionally be heard slamming shut, and strange footsteps that were not those of the other men on duty could be heard. "It was pretty spooky," said Rocha. "Even though this wasn't the hospital where they brought the aliens…that was next door…you still have the sense that something happened around here."

Speaking of aliens, the most extraordinary sighting of something strange at the NMRC happened to the late Josephine Morones, who saw what she called "little man." Others called it the "alien ghost." It occurred in July of 1997, when interest in the Roswell Incident was at its peak. Morones was stepping out of the staff kitchen one night at the NMRC when she was struck with a strange feeling. Turning to look down the hall, she saw a bizarre sight: a small humanoid figure.

"My thing was very weird. The hands weren't like fingers, they were like mittens. All I could see was the thumb. The skin, or whatever it had on, was like silk tape. We have [silk tape here] and it looked to me like someone wrapped up in that silk tape," Morones remembered. When asked whether or not she thought it looked like an alien, she said, "It had the egg/pear-shaped head. You know how people talk about the slanted eyes and all of this? This one had round eyes. It didn't have a nose; as far as a mouth it had a little bitty mouth. At first I thought somebody was playing a trick on me."[2]

Morones also noted that the figure cast no reflection in the glass cabinet it was standing in front of at the end of the hall: "I kept looking at it and I didn't panic because I've known about this place for a long time…but I looked at the glass expecting to see a reflection and what got me was there was no reflection. I kept looking at it and it suddenly just faded out…"

Morones would see the figure again several nights later. "I was walking out of the kitchen, and I got that feeling again and that time I knew what it was. With that in mind, I was able to turn around and look, and it was just standing there again."[3] This time, Morones was able to call for a coworker to come and look at it, too, but by the time she finished calling him, the figure had disappeared never to be seen again.

In summing up her strange encounter, Morones said, "The first time, it freaked me out and I was really afraid. I had heard all these stories and stuff but I never really believed them. I didn't feed into stuff like that. I didn't believe in all the stuff that was going on this building."

In recent years, the NMRC was torn down and replaced with a newer structure elsewhere on the base. The ghosts did not relocate with the staff.

Chapter Notes

---

[1] "Things that go bump in the night," *Vision Magazine* (Oct 2009), p.4.
[2] Personal Interview with the author, January 2008.
[3] Ibid.

21.
GEORGIA REDFIELD'S
UNMADE MOVIE

All writers dream of one day having one of their novels or stories adapted into a major motion picture. The same was true of Georgia Redfield, and while not all writers can compose a story worthy of the big screen, Redfield penned what would've undoubtedly been an epic film of the late 1940s. Entitled "The White Virgin," it took place in two parts and spanned the time of the conquistadors to the atomic era. The backdrop was the Jornada del Muerto, through which Juan de Oñate marched and the atomic bomb was tested. The backbone of the story was a romantic legend popular in New Mexico at the time: the White Lady of the Sands, known in Spanish as Pavla Blanca.

An early-day Roswell writer and newspaperman, Will Robinson, glimpsed the White Lady during a trip to White Sands with Pedro Cassini in the 1930s:

> One evening old Pedro was counting his beads as the sun set in a burst of glory over the San Andres Mountains. "The White Lady will rise again when the moon comes over the Sacramentos," he said. "Twice it will be for me. Once more will be the last, as it was with my father and many others who have seen her."
>
> The wind was coming across the plains of the Sacramentos from the southwest in long, steady flows,

but not so very hard. Most likely it bounced off the prairies at times, and when it struck it moved things.

"There she is," said one of the men pointing to the top of one of the great dunes. Here the wind seemed to be deflected, and high in the air rose a spiral of white, light enough for the mountains to be seen through it, but positive enough that there was no mistaking that the White Lady was walking again in the vast area of alabaster covering 270 square miles. Old Pedro continued to count his beads until the White Lady gathered her fleecy garments about her and vanished into the night.[1]

The White Sands. (HSSNM Larkham Album Three)

The real identity of the White Lady was the fiancé of a conquistador. Her name was Mañuela, and the conquistador was Hernando de Luna, one of Francisco de Coronado's men employed in the search for the fabled Seven Cities of Gold. Mañuela remained in Mexico under the agreement that when the northern Kingdom of New Spain was properly settled, de Luna would send for her to join him. Instead, on the trek across the dreaded Jornada del Muerto, Coronado's men were attacked by the Apache. De Luna became separated from the troop and soon found himself lost among the blinding white sands. Coronado and his men traced de Luna's tracks across the dunes but never found his body. It was as though he disappeared into thin air.

Mañuela headed north into the region upon news of her fiancé's disappearance, escorted by a group of Jesuits. One night, under cover of darkness, Mañuela donned her wedding dress, mounted a horse, and rode off into the sands, never to be seen again—not in corporeal form, at least. As stated before, from then on, her ghostly essence was seen among the swirling sands carried in the winds.

It was from this particular legend that Redfield crafted her story treatment, alternately entitled "The White Virgin" and "The Hour Glass," after the white sands themselves. A press release for the book written by Redfield was as follows:

> Much interest by prominent literary people of Roswell is centered on a forthcoming book nearing completion by Georgia B. Redfield which is based on the history of New Mexico, through the ages from the Cretaceous, near the "age of dinosaurs" – some 60 million years ago...
>
> The story [represented] by a huge hourglass, symbolical of the dry lake bed from which the great White Sands National Monument in New Mexico, evolving through the ages, were formed...

"The screen version has been described by a moving picture producer as the most beautiful screen story he had ever read," Redfield said and she wasn't exaggerating. A letter from the producer, Marlin Wargin, exists and the high points of the letter are as follows:

> I again say that I think your story is a wonderful picture possibility and I personally believe that a picture of this type would have universal appeal. During the past year or so many original outlines for stories, or entire scripts have been submitted to us for consideration for picture productions but none appealed to me as your story based on the colonization of New Mexico, its attractions of national interests, the bomb site, and bomb test. I have read only your outline, so far, however I can visualize the entire story, very clearly, in my mind. I shall

try to arrange a trip to take place within the next two weeks, so that I may present my ideas and plans for the production of the picture.

Redfield's treatment was something of a pastiche of New Mexico history, including everything from the Penitente rotherhood to the super-scientists of Los Alamos. The story was told in two parts, with Part II set in the then-modern era of the 1940s, and Part I during the time of the conquistadors. Part I's heroine, Madeline, was based upon Manuela, the White Lady of the Sands, or Pavla Blanca. In Redfield's story, Madeline was depicted as a prominent maiden from Spain engaged to Captain Carlos Sanchez. It began with the couple's engagement party in Spain before setting off on Oñate's expedition into New Mexico.

Oñate was also a prominent supporting character, and in an early scene, a fortune teller ominously predicted death and disaster for his looming expedition. Despite the doomsday prediction, Oñate leads his party into New Mexico, where Madeline and Carlos are married in an old church. When Carlos later leaves on a buffalo hunt with Oñate, he gets lost and is covered up in a sand storm. Before he departed, Madeline didn't tell him that she was also pregnant. Adding to the trauma, a smallpox outbreak occurs and many in the expedition begin to die. From this, the Penitentes are born, who begin torturing themselves in hopes of warding off the plague. At this point, Oñate dramatically declares it the journey of death, thus naming the Jornada del Muerto. Madeline dons her wedding dress in hopes that Carlos is still alive somehow and sets off into the white sands. She, too, is overwhelmed in a sand storm and is later found by an elderly woman called Mother Squaw. Under the old woman's care, Madeline gives birth to a baby boy and dies. Later, her son is found by members of the expedition, who take him back to Santa Fe, where he is raised under his proper title and becomes a prominent citizen.

Part II jumped into the Atomic era, with a new male lead, Captain Robert F. Busby, speeding up a modern highway adjacent to the Camino Real and the Jornada del Muerto traversed by the conquistadors. He's supposed to perform a daring test flight the next morning, but his careless driving results in him crashing his car. He flags a ride from a passing car and is picked up by two women being escorted by a chauffeur. One is Zora Howard, a beautiful young blonde, and the other woman is her elderly caretaker. Zora is one of the scientists being whisked away to the secret city of Los Alamos to work on the bomb. By the time the duo drops Busby off in Albuquerque, it's clear that Busby and Zora will serve as the romantic leads of Part II. Unfortunately, Redfield's treatment ended with Busby's plane going down, possibly in an act of sabotage, and did not resume. However, her notes stated her story would eventually end with a wedding between Busby and Zora at White Sands, with the ghost of Madeline watching.[2]

Tragically, Redfield never finished the story, and a press release explained that "Mrs. Redfield, a well-known historian and Roswell writer, for the Roswell newspapers, *El Paso Times*, and *New Mexico Magazine*, suffered a serious accident, from which she has been confined to her bed for 10 months. For this reason she has been unable to complete the last two chapters of her book, on which she has been working for the past three years." Sadly, Redfield passed away in 1956, with neither the book nor the film coming to be.

However, Redfield left an indelible impact on the history of New Mexico. For instance, Living New Deal.org surmised, "Redfield's efforts were vindicated after her death, as her WPA manuscripts have informed several history books, on subjects ranging from cattlemen to Billy the Kid."[3]

Chapter Notes

---

[1] Robinson, "The White Lady of the Sands," *Yucca Land*, p.193.

[2] Also figuring into the story was to be a portrait of Madeline, painted on the journey, and which resembled Zora.

[3] https://livingnewdeal.org/sites/georgia-redfield-archive-wpa-new-mexico-collection-fray-angelico-chavez-history-library-santa-fe-nm/ The site explained that Redfield had also authored an entire guidebook to Roswell with "90 points of interest," though only two and a half pages of her work pertaining to Roswell appeared in the *New Mexico American Guide*.

PAT GARRETT

IS KILLED

SHOT TO DEATH BY HIS TENANT, WAYNE BRAZELE, AFTER QUARREL ON HIGHWAY.

WAS A ROSWELL PIONEER

Settled and Improved Eight Hundred Acres of Land East of This City.— Received Greater Notoriety for Killing "Billy the Kid" and Causing Other Desperadoes to Bite the Dust. A Famous Character.

Roswell Daily Record (March 2, 1908).

22.

LOST EVIDENCE
IN THE PAT GARRETT KILLING

On a dusty road outside of Las Cruces in February of 1908, Pat Garrett met a mysterious end. The only witness, a Roswell man by the name of Carl Adamson, claimed Garrett had become violent during an argument with a young goat herder, Jesse Wayne Brazel. When Garrett went for his shotgun, Brazel put a bullet in Garret's head in self-defense. Never mind that a coroner's report later showed that Garrett was shot through back of the head, likely when he had stopped to urinate and was least expecting it.

The fact of the matter was that there were lots of people who wanted Garrett dead in 1908. Over the years, he had acquired numerous friends and foes, though possibly more of the latter considering his untimely end. Among Garrett's more notable enemies at the time were powerful politician Albert B. Fall and even Garrett's own neighbor, W.W. Cox. In the years since he had left Roswell, Garrett had made waves as the Sheriff of Doña Ana County in 1896, when he tried and failed to solve the murder of Albert J. Fountain and his young son, Henry. After that, Garrett even served as Collector of Customs in El Paso beginning in 1902. By 1908, he was down on his luck and living outside of Las Cruces with his family.

Jesse Wayne Brazel, seated in the middle, was indeed related to W.W. "Mack" Brazel who would find the flying saucer debris outside of Roswell in 1947. Through this strange coincidence, the story of the Roswell Incident can be linked to Pat Garrett.

What had begat the fatal feud between Garrett and Brazel was when the former leased land to the latter. Garrett was under the impression that Brazel would let cattle graze on his land, not goats. Goats were a problem because as they grazed, they would eat not only the grass, but also the roots, thus ruining the land. As legal efforts to push Brazel off his land failed, Garrett thought he had found his salvation when Carl Adamson and Jim Miller came calling to buy his land. He was wrong. They were his damnation instead. Miller was in fact the infamous paid assassin Jim "Killer" Miller, and Adamson was a crooked Roswell man who claimed he wanted to buy Garrett's land for some Mexican cattle he and Miller owned. Instead, it later turned out there likely never was any cattle. Supposedly, the duo existed only to bait Garrett into a fateful trap along with Brazel.

Most historians today agree that Brazel was chosen as a likeable fall guy, who was likely to be acquitted in self-defense against Garrett. Instead of Garrett going for his gun during an argument, most concur that Miller, hiding behind a sand dune, shot Garrett in the back of the head along the trail as Garrett urinated.[1] Adamson testified that while Brazel and Garrett were arguing, Garrett went for his gun, and Brazel was quicker on the draw, shooting in self-defense. Brazel was acquitted as planned, but many locals knew better. They knew Garrett had been murdered. But if only they could prove it.

Picking up the Garrett investigation many years later was Robert N. Mullin, who as a boy used to follow Garrett around El Paso in awe. Mullin wrote in his article "The Key to the

Mystery of Pat Garrett": "In my opinion the truth may never be known until and unless comes to light a true copy of the report made by Frederick Fornoff, Captain of New Mexico's Territorial Mounted Police, whose investigations began at the scene of the killing even before the victim was buried."[2]

Pat Garrett in his later years, when he served as Collector of Customs in El Paso.

This report was said to contain new and startling information differing from the official reports. Mysteriously, this report was never utilized in Brazel's trial. If it had, things may have turned out differently. Diligently searching for the missing report, Mullin learned that James Hervey had it all the time, though he chose not to divulge its contents (which still remain a mystery) in a posthumously published *True West* article. Even what was revealed in the article was considered so scandalous that Hervey stipulated it could not be published until a full eight years after his death, which it was in 1961.

Mullin did learn that Judge Charles R. Brice, a former partner of Hervey's in Roswell, had Fornoff's full report. Brice passed away in 1964, and Mullin learned that his papers had all since been destroyed in accordance to his wishes. In October 1968, Mullin spoke with Brice's daughter, Mrs. Evelyn Dowaliby, who told him that she and others in the family had disposed of those papers and records years prior. Specifically, the Judge had felt that if certain papers were made public, a vicious scandal would ensue. Initially the papers were left in a back alley behind the J.P. White Building to be hauled to the dump, only Morris P. Frederick, an employee of Glover's Packing Plant, picked them up out of curiosity. When Brice's heirs learned of this, they tracked Frederick down and saw to it that all the papers, including the invaluable Fornoff report, were burned!

Judge Brice, right, posing with famous
New Mexico lawman Dee Harkey.

Brice in a group photo with Cecil Bonney, whose father may have sold Garrett the bullet that famously killed Billy the Kid. Cecil Bonney had occasion to speak with Brice in his office before he died, and he told Bonney he was certain Miller fired the fatal shot, if that's any indication as to what confirmation the Fornoff report might have held. Naturally, Brazel and Miller weren't the only ones speculated to have done the killing. An old timer named Bill Isaacs speculated that it was Roswellite Carl Adamson himself who had done the shooting and used Brazel's gun to do so. Isaacs shared his theory with Jarvis Garrett, one of Pat's sons, many years later. As such, Jarvis came to believe Adamson was probably the real killer.

Lewis A Ketring, Jr., also said that he spoke to Brice before he died regarding the Garrett case. Ketring visited with Judge Brice at his Riverside Drive home in Roswell in 1958 and remembered to Mullin:

> This was on April 1, and the next day I talked with him again in his office in the [J.P.] White Building. Judge Brice was continuing the law office where he and his friend and longtime partner, James M. Hervey, had practiced together for many years. Judge Brice told me quite frankly that he had in the office files of the [Fornoff] report, the one made for him by the territorial police after the killing of Pat Garrett, but Judge Brice declined "at least for the present," to let me examine or copy it.[3]

155

Roswell's J.P. White Building, where Judge Brice's office was located. (HSSNM #480A).

Is it possible that the long-standing mystery of Pat Garrett's death could have been solved via the Fornoff report, hidden away within the confines of the J.P. White Building? Considering the contents were burned, we will never know.

Chapter Notes

[1] Legend has it that Jim Miller once told a man that Pat Garrett was the closest call he ever had. This tale was told in a written letter to Judge Brice from Tom Coggins, who knew Miller. "Pat had a gun down in the bottom of the buggy by his foot and got it and almost killed Miller. He said Miller said it was the closest call he ever had in any of his killings."
[2] Mullin, "The Key to the Mystery of Pat Garrett," *Los Angeles Westerners Corral* (June 1969), p.1.
[3] Ibid, p.4.

23.
NIGHT OF THE
LECHUZA

Second to La Llorona when it comes to the Land of Enchantment's female specters is La Lechuza, the owl witch. While most all New Mexico witches were accused of turning into owls from time to time to indulge in their nightly prowls, the Lechuza was different. As opposed to a regular owl, it was thought to be a gigantic owl with the face of a woman. Like La Llorona, La Lechuza often targeted unfaithful husbands, drunks, and most of all, young children.

And, while the Lechuza might seem more likely to be spotted in northern New Mexico, one terrorized southeast New Mexico many years ago. Brought to light on an episode of *Monsters and Mysteries of America*, former Roswellite Octavio Ramos related an encounter that his parents had with the owl witch.[1] His parents, Juan and Maria Ramos, emigrated to America from Mexico separately in the 1960s, when they were both in their twenties. As both worked odd jobs in Roswell, they met, fell in love, and got married. The couple wasn't plagued with the Lechuza until after the birth of their son, Octavio.

The first major incident occurred in the Autumn of 1964. As Juan went outside to water some trees on the property, he saw an orange fireball floating from his neighbor's home toward his own house. He called Maria to come see it as well. Apparently not superstitious, Juan thought it may have been a strange meteor of some sort.[2]

Every night following, the fireball would swarm about the house as the dogs howled madly outside. But Juan still had to go out and water the trees at night, as it was his job. While in the barn checking on a generator, he heard a strange commotion. He looked up in the rafters to see about a dozen owls gathered there. A feeling of sheer terror crept over him and he ran back to his house, knowing it was more than just a gathering of owls. As he clutched his gun, he and Maria listened fearfully as the owls walked across the roof of their house. Among them sounded to be either a human being or one giant owl on the rooftop. The large creature made its way down to one of the shudders, which Maria opened in curiosity. Rather than a giant owl, she saw a ghostly shrieking woman not unlike La Llorona. Thankfully, the frightful figure eventually disappeared.

Things escalated when Juan was struck with appendicitis either the next day or a few days later while working in the field. As Juan deteriorated night after night, the owl witch seemed to be lurking outside to taunt the family. Maria called for a local curandera to come and help, and the woman speculated one of their enemies was using the owl witch to try and drive them away. Either that, or the Lechuza was after baby Octavio.

Just as in the old days, Juan was instructed to take a bullet and engrave a cross on it. Though weak with his illness, Juan had to be the one to kill it, said the curandera. Juan took his rifle outside, carefully loaded with the special bullet, and waited. Suddenly, he heard a high-pitched scream, and the witch, in fireball form, was racing towards him. He hit the fireball dead on and it disappeared. Upon inspection, blood and feathers were found in the vicinity of the fireball, but neither the body of an owl or a woman was found. As such, Juan had to wonder if he only wounded the witch and it got away. Whether it survived or not, the Lechuza never returned to torment them again.

Chapter Notes

[1] "Sykesville Monster, Lechuza, The Rake," *Monsters and Mysteries in America*, Season 2, Episode 10 (February 27, 2014).
[2] In New Mexico, in addition to owls, it was believed that witches transformed into fireballs to conduct their nightly flights.

Mrs. Eduardo Rubio Of Lake Arthur Holds Enshrined Tortilla Bearing Image Of Jesus Christ

Maria Rubio poses with the tortilla.
(*Albuquerque Journal*, January 1, 1978)

24.
LAKE ARTHUR's HOLY TORTILLA

The *Roswell Way* magazine once predicted that even though it was "only a few months old," that Lake Arthur "in a few years will be quite a little city. Keep your eye on Lake Arthur." While Lake Arthur never became the city that was prophesied, the world did turn their eyes to Lake Arthur in 1977 for the most unexpected of reasons. That's because, while the Vatican has the Shroud of Turin, Southeastern New Mexico has the sacred tortilla of Lake Arthur. The tortilla, which appeared to have the face of Christ on it, was remembered years later in the September 2004 issue of *American Profile* magazine thusly,

> Since 1977, thousands have visited Lake Arthur (pop. 432) – often bringing photos and prayers of loved ones in need of healing – to see a shrine that Maria Rubio created after a flour tortilla she cooked revealed skillet burns that resembled the face of Jesus Christ.

On October 5, 1977, Maria Rubio was making burritos for her husband's lunch and was using flour tortillas. Maria told the *Albuquerque Jounral*, "I was rolling my husband's burrito and on the last role, I notice something which looked like a face. I just stood there, not moving, because it looked like the face of Jesus. I felt chills all over my body, and I wanted to cry."[1]

Perhaps more mysterious than the tortilla is just how Lake Arthur came to be named when there is no lake in the vicinity. In the booklet *Chaves County Post Offices,* on page 37, it was explained that "Arthur V. Russell was one of the early settlers in the area. He started ranching about three miles north of where the town would be located in very near the lake that would be named in his honor." However, many locals dispute that story. In the article "Say, Lake Arthur, where's the lake?" by Randall Hackley, the author bluntly started the article by stating, "There is no lake and Lake Arthur residents in this little New Mexican community can't remember who Arthur was." The town meter maid was quoted as saying, "A lot of people want to know where the lake is, but we just tell them there isn't one. And when they ask who Arthur is, we have to tell them we just don't know." Another resident, Ray Jones, who owned Lake Arthur's only grocery store at the time, said, "Sorry, no lake. But we have lots of beachfront!" Later, Jones added, "You can drive around town if you want and count the potholes, but there's no lake, and nobody remembers if we ever were named after somebody called Arthur."[2] Only the town clerk, Gerrie Bain, offered a ray of hope that there was ever a lake, claiming that during the era of the artesian wells, there were three lakes in the vicinity of Lake Arthur. In *Place Names of New Mexico,* Robert Julyan noted the presence of a place called Tar Lake south of town. Lastly, some locals alleged that a small basin near town occasionally filled with so much rainwater that they jokingly called it a lake. This basin might be pictured above, as the photo was taken in the Lake Arthur region. (HSSNM #158G)

Maria called for her daughter, Rosie, and she agreed at once that the figure was that of Jesus. Next, she called her husband, Eduardo, and their friend, Mike Salmon, to look at it. They also agreed it had to be Jesus. "Every one of my family felt something," Maria said. She took the tortilla to the church across the street the following day. Father Joyle Finnigan then blessed the tortilla but also told Maria that, in his opinion, what had happened was more or less a coincidence or an accident. "But it's no accident, I know," Maria stated. Before the big piece in the *Albuquerque Journal,* only a couple of papers in the Artesia area had bothered to cover the story.

When *Albuquerque Journal* reporter Jack Coats arrived at the Rubio residence, he noted that the green stucco house looked like most of the homes at Lake Arthur aside from the many cars parked in front of it. He also watched as many people went in and out of the house, some talking excitedly and some "speaking with hushed reverence" about what they had seen inside. By the time of Coats' visit, the Rubios had created a shrine for the tortilla, placed within a glass and metal frame and centered on a table in the dining room surrounded by candles and flowers. At the time of Coats's visit in late December of 1977, 6000 people had been inside the home since October 5th of that same year.

Historical Ozark Trail Marker at Lake Arthur. (HSSNM #765)

The *Journal* article helped spread the word about the tortilla even more so, and soon the home was receiving visitors— Spanish and Anglo alike—mainly from New Mexico and Texas but also from Arizona, Colorado, California, and even a couple from New York City. Many of the visitors asked for Maria to pray for them or they would pray for themselves at the altar of the tortilla.

Before the incident changed her life, Maria was a housekeeper, but since then she began staying home to accommodate the visitors. And just for those wondering, no, Maria did not charge admission for those who came to see the face on the tortilla. She told the *Journal*, "I believe I must show my face to the people and talk to them. I believe the appearance of the Christ is a message for all people to unite with each other as brothers and sisters of God." Maria also said that the incident changed her from an impatient woman to a patient one. A few days after the face appeared on the tortilla, Maria even had a dream where she saw Christ standing in a white robe "with clouds and mist billowing around him."

By 1979, the number of visitors to the Rubio home had exploded to over 35,000. Eventually the Rubios moved the shrine out to a shed in the backyard, but years of heat exposure made the once miraculous image indiscernible. The tortilla met its end when it was taken to a show and tell by Maria's granddaughter for school in 2005. The tortilla was accidentally dropped by someone handling it and it crumbled and broke on the floor. The remains were saved and now reside within a drawer in the family home.

Chapter Notes

[1] Coats, "Image of Christ Turns Home into Shrine," *Albuquerque Journal* (January 1, 1978).
[2] Hackley, "Say, Lake Arthur, where's the lake?" (undated newspaper clipping in HSSNM archives)

APPENDIX I

THE DEATH OF
JAMES PATTERSON

From the Southwest Sentinel *of August 9, 1892.*

GOLD HILL TRAGEDY
Esequel Mena Shot Through the Heart
and James Patterson Fatally Wounded

From Idus L. Fielder, the only eyewitness known to the tragedy, the following particulars were learned: On Saturday last in company with his family, Mr. Fielder went to Gold Hill to inspect the Western Belle gold mine which he owned in partnership with Mr. Patterson, the mine being worked under lease by the last named party. He arrived in the camp about three o'clock p.m.

Mr. Fielder stopped at the house of Mr. Patterson, about 300 yards from the main portion of the village. It becoming known to the miners that the free-coinage champion was in town, they requested him to make a silver speech to them, which he did. Returning from the hall about 9 o'clock in company with Mr. Patterson, the latter gentleman was accosted by the Mexican Mena who had been at work on the mine, and asked to purchase a bottle of whisky for him. He complied and gave him a bottle of whisky purchased at Snyder's saloon. The Mexican had been drinking previously and was in an aggressive mood. He demanded four bottles of whisky which being refused he returned the first bottle to the barkeeper. He continued his demand for four bottles of whisky or money to buy it. The gentlemen proceeded on their way home followed by Mena and another Mexican. When the gate at Patterson's house was reached the Mexicans forced an entrance to the yard despite the efforts of the others to shut the gate and keep them out. They then got between Patterson and the house, pushing him back and frequently slapping him on the breast and in every way trying to provoke Mr. Patterson to resent the obstruction offered to his entrance to his home. During all this time the Mexican Mena kept one hand in his pocket and it is supposed he had a knife ready for use. By the efforts of both gentlemen the infuriated man was pushed aside and Mr. Patterson jumped within the house. Mr. Fielder called to him to open the door which he did and they were both safe for the time being. The Mexicans both decamped in a hurry.

Mr. Fielder told Patterson he had better arm himself as the Mexican acted as if he intended to murder him. He replied he had no arms, whereupon Mr. Fielder gave him a Colt's 45-caliber pistol which he had brought in his buggy and had left on a table in his room when going down town. A few minutes after they thought of the horses in the corral 75 yards away and proceeded thither to see that the Mexicans did not take them, Patterson carrying the pistol in his hand. Returning toward the house they saw Mena run into the yard, and putting his right arm in advance and a part of his body within an open window heard him call twice "Mr. Patterson, Mr. Patterson." Mr. Fielder said, "My God, he is breaking into the house," being much disturbed on account of the unprotected women and children, Mr. Fielder's wife and child being within. The madman hearing the voices ran directly to the men with a pistol in his hand. Mr. Fielder cried out, "Patterson, defend yourself, he has a pistol." The Mexican commenced firing and almost simultaneously so did his opponent.

Patterson struck the Mexican's hand and warded off the first two shots and said he felt certain that he shot the man through the heart before the last two shots were fired, the third shot fired by Mena struck Patterson below the ribs on the left side going completely through the abdominal cavity. The Mexican reeled forward about five steps and fell upon his face dead. Mena had fired three shots, and Patterson two.

Patterson was assisted into the house by Mr. Fielder and physicians from Deming and Silver City sent for Dr. Stovall of Deming being wired for, came down to Lordsburg on the freight train at 2 a.m. and reached the place an hour before Dr. Stephens of Silver City, got there by team. They immediately pronounced his case hopeless, but he realized his condition from the time he was shot, and immediately after the affray made his will and all preparations possible for the arrival of the inevitable spectre, death.

He lived until 5 p.m. on Sunday being conscious the greater portion of the time except when morphine was administered to alleviate his suffering.

James Patterson was an influential and respected citizen of the community in which he resided and his loss will be keenly felt. He leaves a mother, wife and two children, resident of the camp, who have the heartfelt sympathy of the whole surrounding country.

Mena, the murderer, was one of a remnant of the Ascension mob who murdered the Jefe Politico Ancheta last fall. He with others of the same ilk who came with him had been in the habit of going to work with a Winchester rifle on their shoulder, and which they kept close at hand while at work. Everything tended to show a conspiracy to murder Patterson and perhaps others. Two of the gang were placed under arrest, while two others escaped taking with them two of the best horses in the camp, one belonging to Col. Bill Wells. A posse followed in pursuit but failed to overtake them. Wells' horse has since been recaptured at a ranch about 50 miles south and it is expected Mena's partner, who is wanted as an accessory, will soon be captured.

APPENDIX II

VAN SMITH'S DUEL IN THE SUN

From The Santa Fe New Mexican *of June 21, 1876.*

Shooting Affray. — At about 5 o'clock yesterday afternoon, after our Daily had been taken around, the usual quiet of our surroundings was broken into by loud and repeated shots. Supposing that some one was emptying a navy revolver of old loads, we paid no *especial* heed until some person on the street below sung out :"Joe Stinson and Van Smith are shooting at each other in the Plaza."

Hastening down, we arrived in front of the Governor's residence, when we saw Mr. Smith standing on the east side of the Soldiers' Monument in the center of the Plaza, holding a Winchester 16-shooter at rest, as if waiting for some one, all alone, with blood streaming from one of his hands. Col. Willison was the first to reach him, and next came Gov. Arny; to the latter Smith gave up his gun and was led over to his room at the Broad Gauge saloon, and Dr. Gordon immediately summoned to his assistance. Going along with the crowd, we saw blood freely sprinkled about the middle eastern gate of the Plaza, and one of the palings of the fence shattered by a bullet. Across the street from this is Messrs. Fisher & Lucas' Jewelry establishment. On each side of their large show-window the wall had been perforated by bullets, and one had also entered the shutters lying beneath the window, greatly to the alarm of Mr. Lucas, who was at work at his table behind the glass. Next door, south, at the Broad Gauge saloon, another bullet had shattered the sash in the lower north corner of its window. Proceeding again to the monument in the Plaza, we found blood spattered on its eastern front and the indentation of a bullet in the granite panel, high upon its northeastern corner, and also the mark of a glancing bullet in its southeastern corner.

Inquiring the origin and cause of so much promiscuous shooting in one of the most frequented thoroughfares and densely populated portions of Santa Fe, we were informed that Messrs Joseph Stinson and Van Smith had met that afternoon in a saloon, and while there a controversy sprung up between them in which harsh language was used. Both parties were very much under the influence of liquor at the time, and to settle the difficulty Stinson proposed to Smith to meet him at the monument in the Plaza, and fight it out the old way, with pistols. There the parties separated. Smith going to his room and procuring a Winchester rifle, and Stinson arming himself with a navy revolver. Stinson was on the ground first and seeing Smith coming across the street with a rifle, instead of a revolver, commenced blazing away at long range, before Smith reached the gate. Having emptied his revolver, Stinson leisurely walked across the center of the Plaza, to the west, and entered the drug store of Dr. John E. Murphy, Smith firing one or more shots from the Winchester. In this strange duel Smith received two severe, but were are pleased to say, not dangerous wounds, and Stinson escaped without so much as a scratch. One of the balls entered the palm of Mr. Smith's right hand, coming out above the wrist, and the other lodged in his right hip. There are conflicting accounts about Smith's firing, some contending that he fired one or more shots, and others that he did not discharge his piece. Both gentlemen are known as quiet, peaceable citizens, endowed with as much of that article termed "clear grit," as usually falls to the share of Western men; and what astonishes their friends is the fact that such men could plan and carry out so desperate an engagement in the very heart of the city, whether drunk or sober, where the lives of so many disinterested persons were endangered.

Both parties have been interviewed this morning and both are on friendly terms, Mr. Stinson expressing deep regret at the unfortunate turn of an engagement made under the excitement of liquor and without malicious motives. Mr. Smith says he does not recollect anything about pistols being specified, and with the rifle had started toward the monument expecting to meet Stinson and from there proceed to some more secluded trysting-place. He was resting easy under Dr. Gordon's treatment, and with continued good care expects soon to be on the streets again. We are extremely glad that this unfortunate shooting scrape terminated no worse, hoping that for the honor of the fair name that Santa Fe has justly made in late years, that no such scene of blood may ever be again witnessed in her houses or streets; and if it should that the belligerents will go to the top of Baldy Mountain, where no one will be endangered from the stray bullets.

The long continued dry spell of weather and the unusual flow of electricity in yesterday's atmosphere, seemed to have caused a more general warlike desire than usual. We are working out the particulars of several knockdowns said to have occurred.

APPENDIX III

A GLOWING REVIEW OF ROSWELL

From The Las Vegas Daily Optic *of August 22, 1900.*

ROSWELL

The Optic's Special Correspondent Glowingly tells the Tale of the Once Barren Plain, now Made to Blossom as the Rose.

A FERTILE OASIS IN A DESERT
Great Fields of Orchard and Grain Supporting Thousands of Happy Homes.

ETERNAL FOUNTAINS FLOW
Personal Paragraphs and Pertinent Pencilings Penned for the People's Paper.

Up through the bracing, inspiriting air of northern New Mexico, climbing the sublimity of her mountains everlasting which reach into the low-flinging clouds and break them into a precipitation of the western life-god, rain; on through the sunny slopes and plains of Colorado, northeastern New Mexico and Texas, where the green ranges recede until lost in the baffling beauty of the horizon's mirage; travelling this verdant monotony and down the gulf-bending mesas, the weary eye catches sight of an oasis—first apprehended as another mirage, but upon approach the misty spires materialize as the heaven-standing sentinels of handsome churches of every denomination; the filmy parapets become the fringe of magnificent shade, trees, and the fairy lakes and rivers flow in reality from the rifled earth as though obedient to the touch of a magic wand—it's thus that the traveler approaches Roswell, the luxuriously verdant city of southeastern New Mexico. Other towns and cities may cry with the parched lip, but the voluptuous maid of the southeast may drink from her eternal rivers and smile with the wet upon her brow. The arterial vigor of the western world is here; out of the full bosom of the earth springs the eternal fountain with the sweetness of the catcus bloom and mantles it with an extravagant verdure. For the desert, the waving fields appear; for the leafless plain there are bowers for gods; for the silence of space, concourse of sweet sounds in the humming song of industry. The lonely coyote's howl has fled before the laughter of a child; the wild haunt of the outlaw has been transformed into a home by the gentle arts of man, and in the wild court of nature the human suitor has filed a successful application for partition; and water did this—water like that struck from the rock in the story of miracles.

"Gates of brass cannot withstand
One touch of that magic wand."

The lamp of Aladdin has been found; and burnished by the hand of industry, Lo! the waiting genial leave appeared to do its bidding.

The Pecos Valley railway winds through this embowered city as a serpent through a garden, making communication through the Colorado and Santa Fe railways on the north and the Texas Pacific, Southern Pacific, Santa Fe and Mexican Central on the south. Not an unreasonable hope furnishes the prospect of another road through to the Santa Fe at Albuquerque on the west and El Paso on the southwest at no distant day; then, Indeed, will the Innumerable and fruitful gardens and miles or orchards of Roswell scatter their plenty upon the markets of the giant Gate City, and her New Mexico sisters of the west; her vast ranches, within a span of the city limits, some of them containing ten thousand acres, will sweeten their hay mows with millions of tons of alfalfa; her high-grade Herefords will push their snow-white faces into the pastures of a thousand New Mexico farms and carry their noble strain among the herds of a thousand hills. The precincts of the little city offer to visitors the convenience of broad, well-graded streets that touch the lateral hills with the directness of an arrow's ends, and the tired soul is balmed with the umbrageous comfort of limitless "alamos" and the soothing drapery of countless weeping willows; the winding rivers, mysteriously percolating the earth like the welling of silent tears, crystalize the sun's rays into a sheen of silver, and aside from their poetry yield the finny game or bathe the lounging limb every month in the year, and their limpid pools excel the Roman baths of old. Perpetual fountains, released by no less magic than the hand of man, wash the air and play with the sunshine, make the rainbows of hope of the ancients on beautiful yards and farms, invigorate the tired earth and joy the springing grass. This is Roswell, which twenty-five years ago boasted of one lone cabin of a fearless pioneer and the dangerous trail of the plain; when earth had not yet unbosomed the secret of her chambered crystal; when the seeds of her beautiful fruit yet lay in the sap of the eastern orchards, and of her luxuriant alfalfa in the struggling verdure of western fields; when the early progenitors of magnificent herds of thoroughbred cattle nipped the grass of the Missouri slopes; when the soft gentleness of her women and the chivalric daring of her men were embryonic in the spirits of the rugged east and perfumed south. This is where the Apache stole the eagle's swoop and bushwhacked civilization in its swaddling clothes; here flourished the famous and youthful outlaw, Billy the Kid, whose father's name was lost in the appellation of a slang soubriquet, and whose nerve and daring found it's chief exercise in sending souls to unsought eternity or thrust terror into those undeparted, or in playing the modern Robin Hood. The nervous coyote in days gone by, here bayed the moon and cut the throat of the unprotected. But all these terrors are in the night-mared past, and peace has cried her presto!

Think of orchards a mile square; of ranches four miles square, under fence, all in use, supporting 1,000 head of high-grade cattle worth over fifty dollars each, producing a five-cutting crop of alfalfa each season—1,600 tons, valued at $20,000—watered by artesian wells; think of immense acequias running everywhere and full to the banks with water as beautiful as the bottled commercial product of Waukesha, and as large as the "rivers" of the mountainous New Mexico. And when we wonder at these blooded cattle whose progenitors weigh 2,000 pounds and are so fat that the backbone sinks to the bottom of a furrow of loin, though fed no grain, we cannot but also wonder why the agricultural college of New Mexico finds it necessary or excusable to slight her own stock raisers and send to Iowa for cattle for its farm.

He who looks with a practical eye upon the resources of New Mexico, and upon her possibilities, need not feel timorous in this sanguine prophecy: The time will come when we will eat bread from New Mexico wheat, ship vegetables, fruits and meat from New Mexico canneries; wear clothes and shoes made here from New Mexico wool and leather; fashion in New Mexico, from the product of her mines of gold, silver, copper and iron, smelted with New Mexico coal, all the myriad articles useful to domestic, agricultural and mining life and stock our farms with New Mexico bred, high-grade cattle; there will be a grand reciprocity in New Mexico when the hardware, whose raw product shall be wrenched from the rook-ribbed mountains of western, northern and central New Mexico, will exchange for the food-stuffs and luscious fruits of the Pecos, Mesilla, Taos and San Juan valleys; when western and central New Mexico will clothe the shivering, and the wealthy lavish exuberance of the Roswell, Carlsbad and Las Cruces irrigated sections will feed the hungry. And while we enjoy the benefits thus mutually produced, we will look kindly upon the drawn-chested health seeker who flees from the suffocation of the east to this great western sanitarium and shakes off, in this regenerating climate the hand of death, as though prematurely laid in this generous air where the parched body may be recuticled, the soul reinspirited—where life reassumes the sweet gladness of an almost forgotten vitality.

That this reality may not be considered a dream iridescent, the reader may see for himself by going to Roswell on the 9, 10, 11 and 12th days of October coming and attending the Chaves-Eddy and Lincoln county fair— when he may see the truth, whereof it is above written.

BIBLIOGRAPHY

Books

Hispanic Americans in Congress. Committee on House Administration of the U.S. House of Representatives, 2013.

Adams, Clarence. *Three Ranches West.* Carlton Press, Inc., 1972.

Ball, Eve. *Ma'am Jones of the Pecos.* University of Arizona Press, 1973.

Bonney, Cecil. *Looking Over My Shoulder: Seventy-five Years in the Pecos Valley.* By the author, 1971.

Bullis, Don. *Unsolved: New Mexico's American Valley Ranch Murders & Other Mysteries.* Rio Grande Books, 2014.

Fleming, Elvis E. *Captain Joseph C. Lea: From Confederate Guerilla to New Mexico Patriarch.* Yucca Tree Press, 2002.

--------------------*Treasures of History IV: Historical Events of Chaves County, New Mexico.* iUniverse, Inc., 2003.

Fleming, Elvis E. and Ernestine Chesser Williams. *Treasures of History II: Chaves County Vignettes.* Historical Society for Southeast New Mexico, 1991.

------------------------*Treasures of History III: Southeast New Mexico People, Places, and Events.* Historical Society for Southeast New Mexico, 1995.

Fulton, Maurice G. *History of the Lincoln County War.* University of Arizona Press, 1968.

----------------------- *Roswell in its Early Years.* Self-Published.

Klasner, Lily. *My Girlhood Among Outlaws*. University of Tucson Press, 1972.

Kraul, Edward Garcia and Judith Beatty. *The Weeping Woman: Encounters with La Llorona*. The Word Process, 1988.

Metz, Leon. *Pat Garrett: The Story of a Western Lawman*. University of Oklahoma Press, 1974.

Nolan, Frederick (Ed.) *Pat F. Garrett's The Authentic Life of Billy, the Kid*. University of Oklahoma Press, 2000.

Shinkle, James D. *Reminiscences of Roswell Pioneers*. By the author, 1966.

--------------------- *Martin V. Corn, Early Roswell Pioneer*. By the author, 1972.

Snorf, Annie Laurie and Hazel Vineyard (Ed.). *Yucca Land: A Collection of the Folklore of New Mexico*. American Guild Press, 1958.

Twitchell, Ralph Emmerson. *Leading Facts of New Mexican History*. Torch Press, 1917.

Articles

"Things that go bump in the night." *Vision Magazine* (October 2009).

Adams, Clarence. "Did you hightail it for Six-Mile Hill? Where were you the day Roswell was "doomed?" *Old Timers Review* (Vol. 4 No.4.).

Coats, Jack. "Image of Christ Turns Home into Shrine." *Albuquerque Journal* (January 1, 1978).

Crandall, Guy. "We Built a Mesa." *Old Timer's Review* (Vol.1, No.4.).

Gibbs, William E. and Alfred L. Castle. "Maurice Garland Fulton: Historian of New Mexico and the Southwest." *New Mexico Historical Review* (Vol. 55, No.2, 1980).

Koonce, Bob. "The Great Oasis Well." *New Mexico Magazine* (August 1966).

Mullin, Robert M. "The Key to the Mystery of Pat Garrett." *Los Angeles Westerners Corral* (June 1969).

Nelson, Morgan. "James Patterson: First Among the First." *WWHA Journal* (October 2009).

----------- "The Early Spanish Through the Middle Pecos." (Morgan Nelson Collection, Historical Society for Southeast New Mexico Archives)

------------ "The Oasis Ranch." (Morgan Nelson Collection, Historical Society for Southeast New Mexico Archives)

Nolan, Frederick. "Van C. Smith: "A Very Companionable Gentleman." *New Mexico Historical Review* (April 1997).

Videos

"Sykesville Monster, Lechuza, The Rake." *Monsters and Mysteries in America.* Season 2, Episode 10 (February 27, 2014).

INDEX

Adams, Clarence, 103, 111-114

Artesia,NM, 15, 141, 163

Ball, Eve, 43, 45, 48-49, 52, 83, 87, 123, 125, 128, 130

Billy the Kid, 7, 14, 39-42, 49-50, 55-65, 69-70, 82, 90, 107, 123, 125, 128, 130-131, 149, 155, 174

Billy the Kid Springs, 60

Bitter Lakes, 17-18, 95-97

Bonney, C.D., 54-57, 62, 124

Bonney, Cecil, 127, 155

Bosque Grande, 18, 21, 23, 47, 61-62

Bottomless Lakes, 15, 17, 78-87, 96-97, 112

Brazel, Jesse Wayne, 151-155

Brice, Judge Charles, 153-156

Carlsbad Caverns, 86

Carlsbad, NM, 28, 83, 175

Carrizozo, NM, 109, 131, 133

Castaño de Sosa, Gaspar, 17-18

Catron, Thomas B., 72-75

Chaves, Col. J. Francisco, 75-77

Chihuahuita, 104-110

Chisum, John S., 18, 21, 23-24, 37-39, 41-42, 47, 49, 51, 63-64, 68, 73-75, 82-83, 87, 89-91, 99, 107, 126

Chisum, Pitzer, 41

Chisum, Sallie, 39, 42, 126, 128, 130

Clardy Family, 99, 102

Corn, Martin V., 61, 89, 93

Dexter, NM, 14, 140

Diamond Cave, 115-121

Eddy, Charles B., 13, 43, 176

Elkins, NM, 75

Elkins, Stephen B., 73, 75

Espejo, Antonio de, 15-17

Fleming, Elvis E., 7, 17-18, 59, 134

Fort Stanton, NM, 19-20, 37, 39-40, 49, 67, 119

Fort Sumner, NM, 19-21, 61-62, 64, 69, 83, 120, 184

Fountain, Col. Albert J., 25, 151

Fulton, Maurice G., 43, 45, 47, 115, 119, 130-133

Garrett, Patrick F., 13-14, 42, 53-57, 61-65, 68-71, 90, 130, 151-156

Goodnight-Loving Cattle Trail, 21-22, 81

Hagerman, NM, 14, 17-18

Hondo River, 11, 18, 45, 47, 55, 141

Hurd, Peter, 42, 61

J.P. White Building, 153, 155-156

Jones Family, 13, 43-52, 67, 91, 123

Klasner, Lily Casey, 12-13, 123-133

La Llorona, 14, 93, 99-103, 157, 159

Lake Arthur, 7, 14, 161-164

Lea, Capt. Joseph C., 13, 19, 41-42, 51, 59, 61-62, 64, 68, 75-76, 80, 86

Lincoln County War, 37-43, 49, 52, 59, 63, 65, 68, 71,

73, 75, 107, 123, 125, 128, 130, 132

Lincoln, NM, 37-39, 51, 61, 128

Llano Estacado, NM, 56

Lorius Lake, 95-97

Lost River, NM, 61-62, 94-97

Lover's Lane, 88-93

Mesa, NM, 117, 121

Mescalero Spring, NM, 54-57

Metz, Leon, 53, 55-56, 123, 125, 133

Miller, James M., 65, 82-83, 99, 152

Missouri Plaza, NM, 44-47, 105

Mullin, Robert, 152-153

Nelson, Morgan, 15, 17-19, 21, 99

Nolan, Frederick, 42, 74, 75

Oasis Well, 99-103, 179

Orchard Park POW Camp, 93, 140-142

Pat Garrett Dam, 55

Patterson, James, 11, 19-28, 42, 73, 165-167

Pecos River, 15-18, 43, 45, 49, 52, 67, 79, 83, 99-100, 134, 175

Picacho, NM, 124-127

Poe, John W., 90, 130

Poe, Sophie, 129-130, 132

Redfield, Georgia B., 7, 55-59, 61, 78-79, 83, 85, 87, 89, 95-97, 105-110, 145-149

Rio Hondo (Spanish settlement), 105

Roswell Incident, the, 7, 29, 135, 143, 152, 184

Rubio Family, 160-164

Saint Mary's Hospital, 135-138

Salt Creek, 17-18

Santa Fe Ring, 9, 73-77

Seven Rivers, NM, 13, 42, 43, 48-50, 52, 67

Silver City, NM, 25, 28, 65, 67, 69, 166

Six-Mile Hill, 111-112

Smith, Roswell, 10, 12, 74

Smith, Van C., 10-12, 14, 23, 29-36, 38, 48, 62, 73-74, 77, 105, 168-169, 179

South Springs, 21, 39, 42, 82

Spring Rivers, 2, 14, 16, 19, 23

Upson, Ash, 11, 38-46, 48, 51, 56-57, 59, 65-71, 74, 77

Walker Air Force Base, 139-144

White Oaks, NM, 25, 59, 61

White Sands, NM, 25, 145, 147, 149

White, J.P., 57, 90

Wild, Azariah F., 59, 62

Williams, Ernestine Chester, 7, 114

ABOUT THE AUTHOR

John LeMay was born and raised in Roswell, NM, the "UFO Capital of the World." He is the author of over 50 books, many of them on the history of the Southwest such as *Tall Tales and Half Truths of Billy the Kid*, and *Roswell USA: Towns That Celebrate UFOs, Lake Monsters, Bigfoot and Other Weirdness*. In addition to non-fiction, he is also the author of the novels *The Noted Desperado Pancho Dumez* and *Once Upon a Time in Fort Sumner*. He is also the editor/publisher of *Strange West Magazine* and has written for Western journals and magazines such as *True West*, *The Coalition Journal*, the *Tombstone Epitaph*, and the *Wild West History Association Journal*. He is a Past President of the Board of Directors for the Historical Society for Southeast New Mexico.

The following titles are available for purchase on Amazon.com, and are available to bookstores at a wholesale discount via Ingram Content Group (ISBNs of available editions listed for this purpose)

CRYPTOZOOLOGY/COWBOYS & SAURIANS

Cowboys & Saurians: Prehistoric Beasts as Seen by the Pioneers explores dinosaur sightings from the pioneer period via real newspaper reports from the time. Well-known cases like the Tombstone Thunderbird are covered along with more obscure cases like the Crosswicks Monster and more. Softcover (357 pp/5.06" X 7.8") Suggested Retail: $19.95 ISBN: 978-1-7341546-1-0

Cowboys & Saurians: Ice Age zeroes in on snowbound saurians like the Ceratosaurus of the Arctic Circle and a Tyrannosaurus of the Tundra, as well as sightings of Ice Age megafauna like mammoths, glyptodonts, Sarkastodons and Saber-toothed tigers. Tales of a land that time forgot in the Arctic are also covered. Softcover (264 pp/5.06" X 7.8") Suggested Retail: $14.99 ISBN: 978-1-7341546-7-2

Southerners & Saurians takes the series formula of exploring newspaper accounts of monsters in the pioneer period with an eye to the Old South. In addition to dinosaurs are covered Lizardmen, Frogmen, giant leeches and mosquitoes, and the Dingocroc, which might be an alien rather than a prehistoric survivor. Softcover (202 pp/5.06" X 7.8") Suggested Retail: $13.99 ISBN: 978-1-7344730-4-9

Cowboys & Saurians South of the Border explores the saurians of Central and South America, like the Patagonian Plesiosaurus that was really an Iemisch, plus tales of the Neo-Mylodon, a menacing monster from underground called the Minhocao, Glyptodonts, and even Bolivia's three-headed dinosaur! Softcover (412 pp/ 5.06"X7.8") Suggested Retail: $17.95 ISBN: 978-1-953221-73-5

UFOLOGY/THE REAL COWBOYS & ALIENS IN CONJUNCTION WITH ROSWELL BOOKS

The Real Cowboys and Aliens: Early American UFOs explores UFO sightings in the USA between the years 1800-1864. Stories of encounters sometimes involved famous figures in U.S. history such as Lewis and Clark, and Thomas Jefferson.Hardcover (242pp/6" X 9") Softcover (262 pp/5.06" X 7.8") Suggested Retail: $24.99 (hc)/$15.95(sc) ISBN: 978-1-7341546-8-9\(hc)/978-1-7344 730-8-7(sc)

The second entry in the series, *Old West UFOs*, covers reports spanning the years 1865-1895. Includes tales of Men in Black, Reptilians, Spring-Heeled Jack, Sasquatch from space, and other alien beings, in addition to the UFOs and airships. Hardcover (276 pp/6" X 9") Softcover (308 pp/5.06" X 7.8") Suggested Retail: $29.95 (hc)/$17.95(sc) ISBN: 978-1-7344730-0-1 (hc)/ 978-1-73447 30-2-5 (sc)

The third entry in the series, *The Coming of the Airships*, encompasses a short time frame with an incredibly high concentration of airship sightings between 1896-1899. The famous Aurora, Texas, UFO crash of 1897 is covered in depth along with many others. Hardcover (196 pp/6" X 9") Softcover (222 pp/5.06" X 7.8") Suggested Retail: $24.99 (hc)/$15.95(sc) ISBN: 978-1-7347816 -1-8 (hc)/978-1-7347816-0-1(sc)

Featuring cases the authors missed, *The Lost Cases* covers things such as the skyquakes recorded by Lewis and Clark, airships and the Spanish American War, Pancho Villa and crystal skulls, lost alien tribe of the Tundra, invisible alien monsters, the Great Moon Hoax of 1835, hellhounds and airships, the Sonora Airship Club and more. Softcover (252 pp/5.06" X 7.8") Suggested Retail: $18.99 ISBN: 978-1-953221-55-1

Cowboys & Saurians: Dinosaurs Down Under takes the series to Australia to explore tales of the cattle devouring Burrunjor, the dreaded Diprotodon, the terrible Tantanoola Tiger, the marsupial Sasquatch known as the Yowie, plus Thylacines, Bunyips, giant rabbits, Megalodons and dinosaurs in nearby New Zealand. Softcover (240 pp/ 5.06" X 7.8") Suggested Retail: $14.95 ISBN: 978-1-953221-34-6

As the title suggest, Cowboys & Saurians in the Modern Era takes the series into the 20th Century with tales of the Texas Pterosaur flap of 1976, the Bladenboro Beast of the 1950s, the Busco Turtle Beast of the 1940s, dinosaur sightings in the Great Depression and far out tales of mini-mastodons, dinosaur men, and Snallygasters. Softcover (320 pp/ 5.06" X 7.8") Suggested Retail: $19.95 ISBN: 978-1-953221-22-3

Settlers & Serpents wrangles the best "Snaik Stories" of the Southwest and beyond in a single volume. Whether it's simple giant snakes or lake serpents, they're corralled in the pages within. Also included are entries on the Leviathan in Mesoamerica and the Southwest plus a detailed look at the giant rattlesnake of Pecos Pueblo. Softcover (180 pp/ 5.06" X 7.8") Suggested Retail: $14.99 ISBN: 978-1-953221-21-6

Written for young readers ages 9-12, Monsters of the Old South collects the best creature stories of the swamplands including White River Monster, Green Eyes, the Crocodingo, the Averasboro Gallinipper, the Tennessee Snake Woman, the Arkansas Gowrow, Bigfoot in the Mississippi River and more. Softcover (122 pp/4.25" X 7") Suggested Retail: $12.99 ISBN: 978-17347816-9-4

Early 20th Century UFOs kicks off a new series that investigates UFO sightings of the early 1900s. Includes tales of UFOs sighted over the Titanic as it sunk, Nikola Tesla receiving messages from the stars, an alien being found encased in ice, and a possible virus from outer space!Hardcover (196 pp/6" X 9") Softcover (222 pp/5.06" X 7.8") Suggested Retail: $27.99 (hc)/$16.95(sc) ISBN: 978-1-7347816-1-8 (hc)/978-1-73478 16-0-1(sc)

UFOs in the Roaring Twenties takes a look at UFO sightings in the 1920s just as the title suggests, along with accounts of Mothman in Nebraska, Lincoln LaPaz's first UFO case, Men in Black investigating an airship crash in Braxton County, West Virginia, Camden's Cosmic Sniper, and much more! Softcover (248 pp/5.06" X 7.8") Suggested Retail: $19.99 ISBN: 978-1-953221-51-3

UFOs of the Turbulent Thirties concludes the authors' investigation of the last unexplored decade of Ufology in the Great Depression with accounts of Mothman, Ghost Fliers, Nazi Bells, the Underground City of the Lizard People, a vanished village on the tundra, and even gangsters and aliens. Softcover (212 pp/5.06" X 7.8") Suggested Retail: $17.95 ISBN: 978-1-953221-35-3

Written for young readers ages 9-12, Space Monsters of the Old West collects the best alien sightings of the Wild West including Mummies from Mars, Bigfoot from the Moon, Pascagoula's space ghouls, the Crawfordsville Monster, Spring-Heeled Jack, Blobs from space, and even the dinosaurian alien creatures that invaded Van Meter, Iowa. Softcover (120 pp/4.25" X 7") Suggested Retail: $12.99 ISBN: 978-1-953221-87-2

Cowboys & Monsters features potentially true stories of real vampires, werewolves, and even mummies unique to America's Wild West period. Examples include the cursed mummy of John Wilkes Booth, New Orleans immortal vampire Jacques St. Germain, precursors to the Beast of Bray Road, and the origins of Skinwalker Ranch. Softcover (316 pp/5.06" X 7.8") Suggested Retail: $19.99 ISBN: 978-1-953221-46-9

The first entry in this trilogy of non-fiction terror sinks its teeth into the lore of the vampire in North America and Mexico, with detailed rundowns on the vampire hunters of Exeter, Rhode Island, a tribe of Bat People, the nocturnal shape-shifting vampire witches of Tlaxcala, the immortal ways of Comte St. Germain in New Orleans and more. Softcover (200 pp/ 5.06" X 7.8") Suggested Retail: $12.99 ISBN: 978-1-953221-38-4

Mummies of the Americas explores Death Valley's city of the Dead, King Tut's Tomb along the Arkansas, the Egyptian City of the Grand Canyon plus the famous mummies of John Wilkes Boothe, Elmer McCurdy, the Cardiff Giant, the Mummy of Helldorado, and even Billy the Kid's pickled trigger finger! Softcover (200 pp/5.06" X 7.8") Suggested Retail: $12.99 ISBN: 978-1-953221-37-7

Cowboys & Dogmen is devoted to tales of werewolves of the Wild West including the dreaded Navajo skinwalker, the Watrous Werewolf, the Beast of the Land Between Lakes, the Hellhounds of El Dorado Canyon, the dreaded Dog Eater, the Wahhoo, the Wolf Man of Versailles, the Michigan Dog-Man and more! Softcover (212 pp/5.06" X 7.8") Suggested Retail: $12.99 ISBN: 978-1-953221-36-0

The first novel from historian John LeMay weaves a fantastic web of fiction via real life mysteries and legends of New Mexico, namely the puzzling theft and return of Billy the Kid's tombstone in 1976, the legend of the Lost Adams Diggings, the villainous Santa Fe Ring, and the enigmatic Acoma Mesa. Softcover (250 pp/5.5" X 7.5") Suggested Retail: $14.95 ISBN: 978-1-953221-42-1

The year is 1950, and old timers connected to the long-dead outlaw Billy the Kid are turning up murdered in New Mexico. Some blame the killings on the avenging witch of the Navajo nation, the skinwalker, while others think it's no coincidence that a man claiming to be a surviving Billy the Kid is set to meet with the governor soon... Softcover (260 pp/5.5" X 7.5") Suggested Retail: $16.95 ISBN: 978-1-953221-32-2

Roswell, USA, the long-forgotten debut work of John LeMay, is available again and covers the minutia of the infamous Roswell UFO Crash of 1947. Notable chapters include tales of an alien ghost haunting the old airbase, monsters in the nearby Bottomless Lakes, and even a dinosaur sighting outside of town. Softcover (248 pp/6" X 9") Suggested Retail: $14.95 ISBN: 978-0-9817597-5-3

This biography, for the first time ever, tells the history of western journalist Ash Upson, who ghostwrote Pat Garrett's *The Authentic Life of Billy the Kid* in 1882 and also reproduces many of Upson's letters that detailed the harsh realities of frontier life in New Mexico during the turbulent Lincoln County War. Softcover (318 pp/5.5" X 8.5") Suggested Retail: $16.99 ISBN: 978-1953221919

ALSO AVAILABLE

From the author of *The New Mexico Book of Witches*

LA LLORONA

Her Kith & Kin

JOHN LEMAY

Tales of terror from the Southwest!

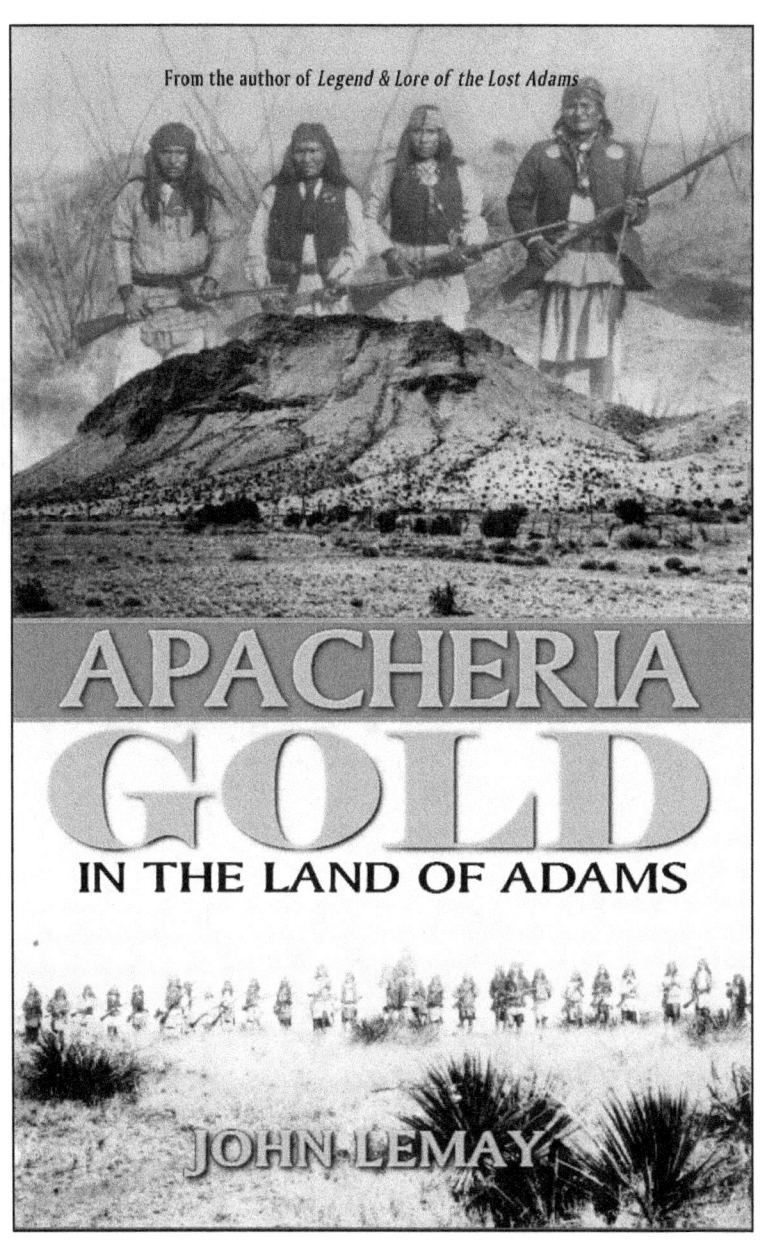

From the author of *Legend & Lore of the Lost Adams*

APACHERIA

GOLD

IN THE LAND OF ADAMS

JOHN LEMAY

NEW MEXICO'S
LOST WORLDS
& ENCHANTED LANDS

JOHN LEMAY

www.ingramcontent.com/pod-product-compliance
Lightning Source LLC
Chambersburg PA
CBHW060929120626
46557CB00003B/933